PIANO DECOMPOSITIONS

Art after Nature

Giovanni Aloi and Caroline Picard, Series Editors

Estado Vegetal: Performance and Plant-Thinking
Giovanni Aloi, Editor

Architecture and Objects
Graham Harman

Piano Decompositions: The Ecology of Destroyed and Decaying Instruments
Heidi Hart and Beate Schirrmacher

Eco Soma: Pain and Joy in Speculative Performance Encounters
Petra Kuppers

Cinemal: The Becoming-Animal of Experimental Film
Tessa Laird

The Lichen Museum
A. Laurie Palmer

Art and Posthumanism: Essays, Encounters, Conversations
Cary Wolfe

PIANO DECOMPOSITIONS

The Ecology of Destroyed and Decaying Instruments

HEIDI HART AND
BEATE SCHIRRMACHER

Art
after
Nature

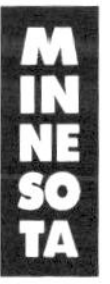

University of Minnesota Press
Minneapolis
London

Open access for this book has been made possible with funding from the Linnaeus University Library and the Linnaeus Center for Intermedial and Multimodal Studies.

Published by the University of Minnesota Press
111 Third Avenue South, Suite 290
Minneapolis, MN 55401-2520
http://www.upress.umn.edu

ISBN 978-1-5179-1936-8 (hc)
ISBN 978-1-5179-1937-5 (pb)
ISBN 978-1-4529-7458-3 (Manifold)

Available as a Manifold edition at manifold.umn.edu.

A Cataloging-in-Publication record for this book is available from the Library of Congress.

Printed in the United States of America on acid-free paper

UMP BmB 2026

The intricacy of the thing we're stumbling over, sawing to pieces, digging up and flooding, or draining; the harmony of what existed in the Rockies, before we got hold of the piano.

—RICK BASS, *THE BOOK OF YAAK*

I made the phone call then, and a kind man
came with his rope and harness. I paid him
to take it in his truck to sink to earth
in the Camden dump. That was August:
it will rot in winter.

—JOAN LARKIN, "NO ONE WANTS THEM"

CONTENTS

INTRODUCTION

During the historic 2024 rains in Southern California, a nineteenth-century grand piano, caked in mud, branches, and debris, landed upside-down in a street. It had tilted out a window when a mudslide pushed a house off its foundation in Los Angeles. The Blüthner piano now resides in an art gallery as an artifact that evokes "beauty even in the wreckage," with implicit reference to climate disasters.[1] It is one of many family pianos lost with all their attendant memories—for example, in the western North Carolina floods caused by Hurricane Helene in 2024.[2] This broken-down instrument, violently reclaimed by natural forces, also recalls pianos either abandoned or intentionally decomposed over the past century.

In this book, we bring current environmental perspective to mid-twentieth-century artworks that involve burning, drowning, or decaying pianos. The continuing fascination with ruined or damaged instruments today, when fewer children take music lessons and more pianos are finding their way to landfills in privileged countries like the United States,[3] shows the instrument's power to carry cultural freight, whether as a vehicle for nostalgia or as an artifact in a time of ecological crisis and collective questioning of what civilization means. We trace this fascination back to the 1960s and 1970s, a time of artistic experimentation and similar questioning, in our focus on composer Annea Lockwood's *Piano Transplants.* These works continue to find new iterations in live and filmed performances. During the Covid-19 lockdown, an extended watch party brought Lockwood's burning pianos, as well as related sequences of pianos placed in a pond or in the forest, back to life in a new era of ecological, political, and public health crises.[4] Witnessing an upright piano slowly burn until its inner metal harp is exposed, seeing forest plants overtake a baby grand piano in the summer heat, or listening to a piano half submerged in a pond is different from listening to music in a concert hall, at home, or via headphones. Instead of the pleasure of hearing either new or familiar sounds, we become aware of the instrument itself and its disruptive treatment. Audience members might feel a mix of discomfort and pleasure; if not used to this kind of performance, they might wonder why anyone would intentionally damage a musical instrument in the first place. For a primarily listening audience used to conventional music, piano destruction (and the thumping, crashing, or untuned sounds that result) might come across as an unraveling of the auditory order.

Artworks like Lockwood's *Piano Burning* and *Piano Drowning* beg larger questions. What does it mean to burn or drown a culturally weighted instrument like a piano—or to risk playing it, however out of tune? The intentional destruction of instruments can cause strong and widely varied reactions (even in a fictional framework). A 2024 Apple ad showing a trash compactor reducing a piano and art supplies into the sleek, flattened surface of an iPad led to intense critique over the company's apparent disdain for cultural work and heritage. In the end, Apple apologized and pulled the ad. This compression of art into screen simulacrum led to "visceral" responses (partly because the ad itself was well crafted as a piece of marketing[5]) but did not invite the cathartic if ambivalent pleasure of smashing instruments in moments of artistic abandon. When artists engage with musical instruments, something more happens. Jimi Hendrix's famous guitar burning in 1967; Kurt Cobain's smashed Fender Stratocaster; Tori Amos's burning piano in promotional photos for her *Boys for Pele* album; Lady Gaga's apparently unscathed emergence from a piano on fire in 2009—through examples like these, the demise of instruments in popular music has its own history of evoking danger and empowerment. Drowning or overgrown instruments appear in popular music culture as well; Taylor Swift's clinging to a flooded baby grand in her "Cardigan" video evokes a sense of needing music for survival, while her performance on a moss-covered piano creates a more benign, fairy-tale atmosphere.

For all its performative power, and beyond the Apple ad controversy, intentional instrument destruction in different contexts can incite pain, even despair. A much-publicized incident of the Taliban burning an Afghan musician's drums and harmonium, alongside the ongoing plight of musicians facing censorship in Iran, has led to outrage in the face of religious extremism and autocracy.[6] As a result, support organizations such as Save Young Musicians have helped promising students from Afghanistan emigrate and pursue their careers in Europe.[7] Acts of ideologically based instrument destruction are not new. They recall Maoist antipiano propaganda (framing the instrument as a bourgeois indulgence) during the Cultural Revolution, a 1917 episode of Bolsheviks dragging pianos through the streets like French aristocrats in tumbrels,[8] Christian churches' destruction of musical instruments in eighteenth-century Britain,[9] and philosophical arguments (going back as far as Plato) for distrusting music's power to affect the body—and the body politic.

While less threatening than instrument destruction under a rigid political regime or even during a rock concert, decomposing a piano in performance art can incite strikingly varied reactions. A classical musician might recoil when a piano burns, depending on the instrument's quality; a folk musician used to fiddle-burning festival rituals might find the experience celebratory; contemporary artists might find the act commonplace if exposed to previous experiments with instrument destruction. From another perspective, a colonialized observer might feel relief after having been forced to march into school to the sound of European classical music.[10] In a time of climate emergency, others might question the basic value of human culture and music or wonder why a burning piano may incite a stronger reaction than wildfires seen on the news. Researchers point out that when musical instruments are destroyed as part of an artwork, this action is qualitatively different from assaults on other material objects or tools.[11] They disagree on what causes affective reactions to these acts, often without additional reflection on the instruments' materiality in larger contexts of human culture and more-than-human entanglement.

Performance artworks like Lockwood's *Piano Burning*, *Piano Drowning*, and *Piano Garden* (in which the instrument decays amid deciduous foliage) inhabit an ambiguous space between contemplative or immersive aesthetics and the dystopian mode in environmental art.

This book shows how this ambiguous position also collapses conventional binaries between music and noise, destruction and repair, and culture and nature. In the process, conventional expectations of musical performance and media communication also collapse. Lockwood's works instead foreground the material transformation of human-made instruments and offer an experience of ecological relationality. These artworks highlight the piano's cultural and material freight in new contexts of fire, forest, and water.

Artistic practices of piano burning and other forms of instrument destruction have a longer history than might be expected. Before Hendrix, Cobain, and mid-twentieth-century avant-garde artists, folk and military traditions included burning instruments, and Laurel and Hardy's 1932 *The Music Box* famously portrayed a player piano damaged through a series of comic mishaps (and taking on its own independent movements outside human control). In works like Annea Lockwood's, humans may set the destruction in motion, but the instruments' exposure to the elements is what breaks them down. Thus, piano decomposition has taken on new meaning in this time of climate crisis and heightened awareness of ecological entanglements. These works recall not only destructive practices but also older instruments such as the water-driven hydraulis (an instrument with pipes and keyboard dating from as early as the third century BCE) and Baroque organ pipes using water to make bird sounds, thus making explicit links with elemental forces. More recent experiments with instruments such as the Wave Organ in San Francisco or toy pianos played with water and stones echo these earlier art forms while taking on new urgency today. Many of these works call attention to what Elin Kahnov calls "nature-culture," which collapses the perceived binary between the two when considering phenomena like performing birds or a "tree opera" that includes the forest's sounds.[12] Likewise, a piano responding to fire or water muddies that distinction and invites human observers to become more entangled in the process too.

Our book does not serve as a catalog of the many works involving piano destruction or decay, but we demonstrate how these works move past mere provocation, inviting engagement with ecological crisis and greater criticality toward cultural tropes and objects usually taken for granted. We have chosen to focus on burning, drowning, and decaying pianos because they unfold multiple meanings, especially in a time of increased ecological awareness. Pianos damaged as the direct result of climate emergency (as in the case of the Los Angeles mudslide or the North Carolina floods) haunt our project, though we concentrate on artworks that experiment intentionally with the effects of fire, water, and weather. We use the term *renatured* to describe instruments placed outdoors in a broad sense because adjectives like *ruined, neglected, devastated,* or *nature prepared* have taken on particular connotations in communities that work with these instruments, such as a piano-salvage operation in the Australian bush or experiments playing toy pianos with stones attached in a stream.[13] We use the term *decomposing* to indicate more specific projects that intentionally disturb received notions of musical composition in favor of more ecologically embedded, compost-like transformations. We also distinguish between *destruction* (in the sense of intentionally setting a piano on fire) and *decay* (in the more passive sense of placing an instrument outdoors for an extended time).

Our book is structured diffractively, approaching piano decomposition from several historical viewpoints and media theories. This approach highlights the ambiguity of destroyed or decaying instruments, depending on their cultural and artistic context. On one level, a performance like Annea Lockwood's *Piano Burning* reduces a cultural artifact to its materiality as wood and therefore fuel for fire; this is shocking in a way a burning cupboard would not be. But on another level, a piano left outdoors suffers the decay implicit in the life cycle of a tree. Questions of sustainability (wood cut from forests or plantations) and colonialist extraction (ivory used for keyboards before the 1940s) haunt the very history of the piano. Recontextualizing a musical instrument in a pond or forest, subject to rain, insects, and overgrowth, is not as forceful as burning but is equally damaging to the instrument over time, even if it already involves what Annea Lockwood sought out as a "truly defunct piano."[14] In all of these cases, multisensory witnessing of the piano's demise is as important as listening to its sounds, as the effects of natural elements through time expose the instrument's inner workings bit by bit. On a cultural level, the artworks draw attention to what Kyle Devine calls "musical exceptionalism" and "commodity fetishism" around instruments like the piano, particularly amid current concerns about Eurocentrism and white supremacy in the classical music tradition.[15] On an ecological level, they invite questions of waste (the sheer bulk of instruments no longer used in human households), toxicity (lead in piano surfaces or keys), and transformation (piano wires sold as scrap metal; pieces of the instruments repurposed to make cabinets or garden planters).[16] On a metaphorical level, they enact burning and drowning to reflect the reality of fires and floods resulting from human-caused climate change.

Annea Lockwood's own idea of "piano transplants" into unlikely settings complicates her works in a productive way, as human-worked materials are recontextualized and transformed into their basic elements of hardwood, basswood, steel, iron, copper, leather, and felt. Lockwood envisioned her works as metaphorical extensions of human heart transplants.[17] In this imaginative leap, subjecting a piano to fire or water is more transformative than violent. The works relate to a subculture around already ruined pianos in Australia, from histories of the instruments as nineteenth-century colonialist transplants (much like the instrument dragged ashore in Jane Campion's New Zealand-based film *The Piano*) to an outdoor sanctuary for cast-off pianos and the "post-musical" works played on them.[18] The idea of sounding ruined pianos has also informed electronic works such as Natasha Barrett's 2019 *The Weathered Piano (quattuor tempora anni),* which creates acousmatic sounds—with no clear source—to evoke the effects of climate-disrupted weather.[19]

Pianos outside their expected habitat take on a haunting quality, especially if they are in a state of disrepair. In a time when pianos are no longer a fixture in many households and instruments often become a burden to those inheriting them, social media images of landfill rescues or upcycled pianos have created an online niche. In addition to texts and films about the ruined-piano subculture in Australia, a recent study entitled *The Lost Pianos of Siberia* traces the remains of what was once a Soviet project to encourage collective artistic training in the hinterlands.[20] And the public display of broken and upcycled pianos aided in a successful 2024 effort to save an acoustically prized concert hall in Salt Lake City from planned demolition to make room for a sports-entertainment complex.[21] When passersby can touch and play instruments that have outlived their indoor capacity, they may better understand not only the fragility of undervalued art forms but also, as an unintentional benefit, the materiality of an instrument that is more a part of the natural world than they may have realized. This process of exposure and breakdown invites a more ecologically attuned sense of what a musical instrument can be.

Theoretical Approach

Our project links questions of cultural affordances with ecomusical materiality in a time when ecocritical fields are moving beyond analysis of human-made works that happen to refer to the natural world. Over the past decade, ecomusicology has pushed boundaries of traditional analysis to ask how listening and sound-making could become more humbly related to the world of which we are only a part.[22] In the related field of sound studies, recent projects that question anthropocentric and colonialist approaches include Mark Peter Wright's *Listening After Nature,* which argues for a more open, less extractivist method of field recording that does not attempt to "capture" other species' sounds;[23] Budhaditya Chattopadhyay's *Sound Practices in the Global South,* which takes a "plurilogue" approach to non-Eurocentric listening and music-making practices through a series of interviews;[24] and Salomé Voegelin's *Uncurating Sound,* which untangles colonialist tendencies in curatorial practices and speaks for "affective knowledge possibilities" through sound as *"being with"* rather than "being music."[25] All of these studies are part of a larger-scale reconsideration of human culture on earth, with implications in aesthetic philosophy as phenomenological and even vegetal entanglement,[26] environmentally grounded curatorial practice,[27] and art history with a growing focus on climate and biodiversity.[28]

Our project builds on these growing areas of inquiry and at the same time adds to studies of musical instruments that sometimes, but not always, explore their ecological relatedness. Though materiality has been a key element in ecocriticism for several decades, with extensions into ecomusicology, these fields still call for an in-depth study of the surprisingly persistent phenomenon of decomposing pianos. While the 2022 anthology *Rethinking the Musical Instrument* includes historical studies of pianos and harps, along with analyses of digital extension practices, it does not make explicit links between instruments and their ecological source materials and sound-making potentials outside the concert hall.[29] *Sound Actions,* Alexander Refsum Jensenius's reconsideration of musical instruments also published in 2022, links digital sound technologies with human embodiment and affect, assuming an anthropocentric position in its treatment of musical "biomechanics."[30] This text also implies a digital ascendance that does not account for the ongoing fascination with weathered and deconstructed analog instruments. On the one hand, the 2023 anthology *Sounds, Musics, Ecologies* includes a chapter on "ecoörganology," or the study of instruments in ecological contexts, but it focuses on digital portable music players rather than on acoustic instruments.[31] Stefan Östersjö's 2020 *Listening to the Other,* on the other hand, describes his practice of releasing violins and guitars into outdoor settings, so that they become mediators and listening agents in a more-than-human context,[32] a shift that this book investigates as well. Topically focused studies of instrument destruction, on the spectrum of political repression to guitar smashing, inform our project,[33] as do our previous collaborations on music and violence used in film and literature to communicate complexity. We have also argued that art addressing ecological crises draws on the ambiguous potential of music and sound to foster audiences' experience of "nature-culture."[34] This book applies our earlier research toward instruments themselves while adding intermedial, elemental media, and posthumanist perspectives. We also consider recent theoretical work linking intermediality and posthumanism[35] and studies of outdoor instruments as "sound sculptures."[36]

After providing background on the piano's cultural affordances, we discuss the material and medial specificities of the instrument, as well as various affective responses to its destruction or decay. Our in-depth analysis of Lockwood's *Piano Transplants* shows how intermedial relationships among pianos, environment, and human perception perform the work of decentering anthropocentric perspective on musical instruments, with the additional layer of film as mediation. Combining intermedial analysis with a posthumanist framework allows us to show what the transformation of instruments can do in shifting awareness toward ecological entanglement. In our analysis, we explore different forms of media—not only the materials of the piano and the films of Lockwood's works but also in John Durham Peters's sense of the elemental media of air, water, and fire.[37] By taking a third way between intermediality and theories of elemental and radical media, we show how a burned, drowned, or abandoned piano is not simply destroyed but changed into a form of productive refuse, not as "abject" waste in the sense of oil or plastic permeating a damaged planet but as part of an organic cycle of radical re-formation.[38] In examining the media transformation of performance to film in Lockwood's *Piano Burning, Piano Garden,* and *Piano Drowning,* we also consider the appeal of the films' slow aesthetics during Covid-19.

Finally, we make a conceptual shift from performance-oriented to more environmentally grounded instruments, showing how the burning or breakdown of a piano can open the way not only for decomposing instruments but also for reimagining their purpose in a less human-centered world. Some ways musical materials can take on new, less anthropocentric functions include using found materials to create listening tools, so as to better apprehend the life of a river or a tree; playing already ruined pianos to create performances that are based on close listening; or placing musical instruments in unlikely natural spaces to find out how the local ecosystem sounds through them. Our examples include contemporary performance artist Julia Adzuki's *Resonant Bodies* tree trunk strung with piano wires, Stefan Östersjö's collaborations involving violins and guitars left outdoors to respond to ecological effects, and coauthor Heidi Hart's artistic research project subjecting a Gothic harp to humid weather (including a hurricane) in the southern United States. Ultimately, this book argues for the value of ambiguity in questioning traditionally Eurocentric musical representations while at the same time salvaging remnants of their own sensory fire.

Outline of Chapters

Chapter 1 contextualizes Annea Lockwood's work within a longer trajectory of piano destruction and decay in both art-historical and musicological frameworks. We trace the history of intentional piano burning from early twentieth-century military rituals to 1960s Fluxus performances and more recent critiques of Eurocentric cultural history. Mid-twentieth-century land art and interventionist ecological works of the 1980s inform this history, as do the experimental piano compositions of John Cage and George Crumb, leading to current extended-technique piano practices that interrogate how the instrument sounds and what purpose it serves. The history of autodestructive practices in visual and performance art (in particular the work of Gustav Metzger) sheds additional light on piano destruction and decay. We include additional examples of recent artistic projects to deconstruct and reimagine the body of a piano. Finally, an environmental art history perspective aids in understanding the recent resurgence of interest in performances like Annea Lockwood's.

In chapter 2, we answer the question "why destroy/renature pianos?" by describing the piano's hybrid structure (as both a percussion and string instrument), its ecological sources and costs, its complexity of design, and its history of tempered tuning. By approaching the piano as a "radical" or "elemental" medium in itself,[39] we lay the groundwork for our third-way approach to instruments as media that activate intermedial and elemental relationships among beings, objects, and environments. We then trace the instrument's trajectory into nineteenth-century bourgeois homes, its symbolic value as a marker of economic class, its function in gender politics and control, and its colonialist and environmental costs. We include perspectives on the piano's role in places outside privileged homes or concert settings where it takes on different values as an out-of-place object, a symbol of oppressive hegemony, or a source of subversive reclamation. A thorough postcolonial history of the piano, as well as a broad consideration of the instrument in all its manifestations (including jazz and rock), are beyond our project's scope; we focus on the piano's implicit legacy of European classical music and ways in which its colonialist movement has created defamiliarizing effects. We apply perspectives from literature and film to show how the piano has taken on weighty cultural affordances that trigger strong but not consistent reactions.

Chapter 3 applies our previous research on music and violence to violence *on* musical instruments by asking what it means to destroy an instrument. After presenting several studies that seek to understand why smashing guitars and burning pianos leads to strong affective responses,[40] we describe burning instruments under fundamentalist regimes in Iran and Afghanistan as an example of extreme actions on the instrument-destruction spectrum, a range that also relates to contemporary artworks on the history of book burning. We explore the idea of instruments as extensions of the human body and how this connection invites specific responses. In this context, pianos appear less as culturally freighted instruments than as exposed, fragile, sounding bodies. Moving from destruction to the decay of pianos over time, we take a qualified approach to posthumanism in which renatured instruments decenter and deterritorialize human cultural materials. Decaying pianos also signal human culture's tendency toward its own demise, as in Claire Colebrook's thinking on extinction,[41] but with more emphasis on material transformation as a kind of composting than on human parasitism or failure as a species.

Chapter 4 builds on theories of radical and elemental media, in which media appear not only as texts, films, or social media feeds but also, at a more basic level, as water, fire, wood, and metal. We focus on Annea Lockwood's piano works to perform a detailed analysis of the instruments' breakdown and transformation. We also discuss the material, sensorial, spatiotemporal, and semiotic modalities at work in the 2021 filmed versions of Lockwood's *Piano Burning, Piano Garden,* and *Piano Drowning,* applying Lars Elleström's approach to intermediality.[42] Multimodal aspects of the filmed performances (the simultaneous experience of sound, image, and meaning-making) combine with the media transformation of film editing to create a simulated experience of slow time, piano sounds, the instruments' decay, and audience–performer interaction. Our third way between elemental and intermedial media theory shows how different layers of mediation shift perspective on what a musical instrument is and means, while breaking down the music/noise and nature/culture binaries.

Chapter 5 reflects on the various perspectives on piano materiality, destruction, decay, and transformation discussed throughout this book. We then move from decomposition to reimagine Eurocentric performance instruments as salvaged materials for new processes of listening to the more-than-human world. Stefan Östersjö's wind- and water-responsive guitars and violins, Sabine Vogel's experiments with ecologically sensitive flutes, and Julia Adzuki's ash tree trunk strung with piano wires serve as our main examples of more than instruments. We also include a reflection on coauthor Heidi Hart's experiment with a decaying harp in the heat and humidity of North Carolina, where the instrument becomes a site for spiderwebs and insect eggs, as well as detuned sonorities that radically democratize conventional musical scales.

A short coda concludes the book with the idea of *re-membering* to reflect on instruments' reparative potential as ecologically entangled cultural materials. This chapter also includes a description of a live piano-burning event in Denmark, a multisensory experience that confirms such art events as entry points for greater environmental engagement and listening beyond conventional sounds. Decomposing instruments prefigure a future in which human performativity becomes less relevant in the face of larger planetary concerns; at the same time, more ecologically attuned instruments offer new sources of curiosity and pleasure.

1 TOWARD A HISTORY OF DECOMPOSING PIANOS

Pianos appear in outdoor settings or subject to destructive forces in many on-screen fictions. In Jane Campion's 1993 film *The Piano,* a mute Victorian woman's piano accompanies her to an arranged marriage in New Zealand, surviving seawater and salt wind to serve as her voice—until it suffers ax blows from her jealous husband and eventually sinks to the bottom of the sea. In the 2000 film *Billy Elliot,* the title character watches as his father axes his late mother's piano into pieces for firewood, which burns like any other split logs. In the 1990s TV series *Northern Exposure,* a piano burned in a house fire becomes a surrogate for a cow meant to be catapulted in an outdoor art project. It sails through the air to the sound of Johann Strauss's "Blue Danube" waltz, recalling the famous space shuttle sequence in *2001: A Space Odyssey,* and crashes to the ground in a thunder of broken strings, disturbing and thrilling the local townspeople. In the 2018 Japanese anime series *Forest of Piano,* two boys from different backgrounds discover a piano abandoned in the forest; it responds only to a particular human touch and has mysterious healing powers. The U.S. historical series *1883* includes a scene of a piano abandoned—and played to sentimental effect—along a wagon trail in the American West, where a river crossing is too treacherous for heavy personal possessions. In a less serious example, a manipulated video of a piano burning while a costumed Beethoven plays it on the beach serves as a metaphor for overworked film scores or for "hot" musical moments. Whether ironically or not, the burning instrument works to visualize music's affective force.

These filmic examples introduce the mysterious appeal of pianos outdoors or reduced to organic material. Often the renaturing or decontextualizing of musical instruments in film (which exploits the visual aspect of the burning or drowning instrument) communicates something about lost culture, personal relationships, or the power of music under duress. In the case of Taylor Swift's "Cardigan" video, the singer's clinging to her piano in a flood conveys a sense of the instrument as a lifeline. In this and many examples from popular culture, an icon of the European musical tradition is reentangled in the natural world from which it came, but with closer reference to humans than to that larger world. In many cases, the instrument remains miraculously in tune despite exposure to the elements. Still, on a deeper level, showing instruments out of their usual context and sometimes subject to violence, these films no longer treat the piano as an aesthetic tool to perform and create musical sound in a conventional concert or household setting. Instead, the instrument becomes an ambiguous presence subject to the elements and capable of unexpected sounds. The visual aspect of these piano scenes also forces attention toward the instrument as an aesthetic object in itself.

Decomposing pianos appear not only in audiovisual and popular culture, but also in performance art and experimental music. In this chapter, we trace the history of renatured and/or decomposing pianos (whether relocated, found, or destroyed) at the intersection of several artistic and musical histories. Working with pianos in new contexts aims not primarily to perform music but to voice otherwise hidden connections and power relationships. We find several unconventional treatments of musical instruments relevant here. First, we trace cultural rituals of burning pianos and autodestructive tendencies in visual art. We then locate Annea Lockwood's *Piano Transplants* in the context of late 1960s and early 1970s Fluxus and prepared piano performance. We address ruined-piano salvage and resulting improvisational works in Australia—works that further complicate the tension between music and noise. Finally, we reflect on all these works, even those not intended as ecological intervention, from an environmental art history perspective. Each of these strands approaches pianos from a different angle, to help tease out intersecting potentials for meaning. Various histories of renatured and decomposing pianos show the cultural freight attached to an instrument that, in its breakdown, leads to strong and equally varied reactions. Later, in chapter 3, we consider reactions to instrument destruction in other contexts (in rock concerts or by oppressive regimes) outside the world of avant-garde experimentation, with its own privilege that may not be so different from that of the concert hall.

Piano Burning as Ritual and Autodestruction

In a European context, the practice of burning pianos has a surprisingly long and murky history. Military piano-burning competitions in the United States and the United Kingdom began as a way to commemorate the Battle of Britain (against the German air force) by squadrons of mainly American volunteers. This practice involved not only competing for prizes but also smashing and burning pianos. These burnings are rumored to have stemmed from the burning of ships at Viking funerals or perhaps from the Gunpowder Plot in England. They may have commemorated the death of a specifically fine piano player or simply subverted cultural "standards" for RAF officers (the ideal of British pilots as gentlemen apparently included piano lessons for non-upper-class aspirants).[1] No matter which of these explanations is correct, most ritualize the burning in a way that links a specific social group's practices to historical rites of passage. As a form of revolt against enforced cultural standards, the prize-winning, destruction, and burning of pianos are all mixed up in carnivalesque subversion of hegemonic values. We will return later to some of the elements implied here: the instrument as stand-in or quasi-human object, also connected to the person who plays it, and the revolt against cultural hegemony in postcolonial contexts.

In the world of performance art, Annea Lockwood (whose father was an RAF pilot) is not the only artist who has set pianos alight, sometimes with a human pianist at the keyboard for as long as safely possible. When an artist takes up this practice, the burning of a piano no longer serves as a *social* ritual; it becomes a spectacle, intervention, or meditative action, depending on the setting. At the same time, ritual can still function as an aspect of art performance, as in contemporary opera and art installations that encourage passage through "threshold states."[2] From the ritual aspect of Greek theatre to Nietzsche's idea of self-transformation through the tragic chorus, performance and ritual have long been intertwined.[3] In the popular music sphere, Lady Gaga's emergence from a burning piano at the 2009 American Music Awards works as a ritual of transformation, survival, and empowerment. In Antonin Artaud's "theatre of cruelty" sense, destruction is key to the personal and social shifts that performance incites, by causing "the mask to fall" and exposing "the lie" of a false existence. Unlike Brecht's theatre of critical distance, which exposes sociopolitical norms otherwise taken for granted, Artaud's model is more cathartic: "the theater like the plague is a crisis which is resolved by death or cure."[4]

Ritual functions like sacrifice have figured in many musical performances, and not only of the death-metal variety. The burning of a fiddle at the end of the 2024 Harpers Ferry Fiddle Day served as a celebratory ending to an intense folk-music fest, with historical reference to the armory burning there at the beginning of the Civil War. Some musicians reacted with more primal sentiments, however; one commented that "the fiddle gods have been sated!"[5] Sometimes the image of a burning piano can signify ritual sacrifice in a personal way that bleeds into the collective, as in a publicity image for Tori Amos's 1996 album *Boys for Pele,* a keyboard-rich fantasia on the immolation of patriarchal norms.[6] The effigy-burning associations with this image imply that an instrument can stand in for a body, a phenomenon we explore throughout this book. Because the piano carries the burden of high culture along with its physical weight, some destructive works that do not involve burning—such as Danish artist Morten Poulsen's moving a grand piano to the very edge of a raised platform in a concert hall or pushing another into a wall—also expose the effort of shifting that burden in a symbolic, ritual way.[7]

The following artworks reflect piano burning as a passage through physical danger, as well as larger ideological messaging in several cases. Artistic examples of piano burning from the past fifty years include Yōsuke Yamashita's 1973 performance, filmed by graphic designer Kiyoshi Awazu and refilmed in 2008, in which Yamashita improvised on the piano in a firefighter's suit until "the piano stopped making sounds," almost suffocating from the smoke in what turned out to be "a life-or-death battle between the piano and myself."[8] Here the piano becomes almost a body with agency, if imagined as a kind of worthy opponent in a ritual battle. Visual artist Chiharu Shiota's 2011 piano burning as part of the MONA FOMA arts festival treated the instrument more as an inert, if still ceremonial, memory container. This burning took place on a public street in Tasmania, recalling Shiota's childhood memory of a charred piano in a house that had burned down.[9] These projects, concerned with metaphorical aspects of the burning ritual, relate to researcher and composer Stefan Östersjö's 2009 collaboration with Bennett Hogg entitled *Devil's Water,* with footage of "a burning violin floating downstream like a Viking funeral ship."[10] Piano burnings with more intentional sociopolitical messaging include Michael Hannan's 2003 radiophonic work *Burning Questions,* which involved playing Beethoven's "Moonlight" sonata on a burning baby grand piano to test "the cultural politics of auto-destructive music,"[11] and Douglas Gordon's 2012 video installation *The End of Civilization,* in which a burning piano in a wild Cumbrian landscape confronted the piano as a "the ultimate symbol of western civilization."[12]

The term *autodestructive art,* referenced in Michael Hannan's piano work, was developed by German-born visual artist Gustav Metzger as a way of radically interrogating past aesthetic forms after the Nazi period. The disruptive practices of Metzger and other notable postwar artists were a response to the ways in which National Socialism had appropriated German aesthetic traditions.[13] Metzger's philosophy also questioned the egocentrism of the market-driven art world in the face of historical atrocities and ecological crisis.[14] His 1960 *Acid Action Painting* took on the quality of a demonstration, also a form of ritual, as the artist applied hydrochloric acid to white nylon at the Temple Gallery in London. Though Metzger did not burn musical instruments, the autodestructive element in his philosophy not only interrogated past cultural forms in the context of historical atrocities but also performed a contemporary critique against the culture industry (in the Frankfurt School sense) and ecological crisis, specifically by making the maltreatment of nature visible. As a teacher of Pete Townshend, Metzger did influence the smashing of guitars as an autodestructive act in music.[15] In a broad sense, Metzger's approach employs destruction and even "revulsion" toward "transforming people's thoughts and feelings, not only about art . . . but to use art to change people's relation to themselves and society."[16] A 2024 reconsideration of his work, along with that of gunpowder artist Cai Guo-Qiang in Los Angeles, shows a tension between slowly burning or oozing substances and more explosive actions, all of which critique entanglements of capitalism, violence, and ecological destruction.[17]

Different strands of intention and interpretation come into play (and sometimes overlap) in piano-burning performances: metaphorical, sociopolitical, and ecological. Annea Lockwood's pianos work metaphorically in their relation to the "transplant" idea and to global heating in more recent iterations; they also function in a more directly ecological way, as experiments with elemental forces. In all the cases noted above, decomposing a piano works by taking apart and exposing the instrument's structural composition as well as the idea of musical composition that is based on scored notes to be played exactly as written. The autodestructive aspect of fire (once intentionally set by human hands) takes its own course in breaking down the piano's wooden case, exposing the cast-iron frame that holds its wires in tension, ultimately causing the wires to snap. The process also recalls rituals involving fire as a threat to be faced and overcome. Though slower than fire, the force of water also takes on an autodestructive role when a piano is placed in a river or pond. As in a baptism or purification ritual, the water functions as a means of change. It may or may not directly critique capitalist modernity, like the art collective Superflex's 2009 *Flooded McDonald's* or Asmund Havsteen-Mikkelsen's more recent drowning of a 1:1 scale model of a Le Corbusier villa in a Danish fjord.[18] Whatever its attendant meanings, the piano is transformed in a ritual passage from an object of cultural containment to an unpredictable tangle of hammers, wires, and keys. Who knows what sounds will emerge?

Decomposing Pianos in the 1960s Milieu

Annea Lockwood's burning and disintegrating pianos did not originate directly from an explicit position of critique but were certainly informed by the general 1960s' questioning of established cultural traditions. A key element in this period was "a reconsideration of the object of art, a move away from the static and autonomous object towards a practice which, at times, literally moved out of the studio, in an attempt to be more responsive to the world."[19] Though conceptual art was developing at the same time, as a foregrounding of idea over object to the point of "de-materializing" artworks "that would be free of art-world commodity status,"[20] artists like Metzger performed this critique through processes that retained their materiality even when corroding or breaking down. As Synnøve Vik has noted, in Metzger's work, "the transformative practices of materiality and technology make explicit the creative process inherent in all forms of destruction."[21] Though Annea Lockwood was hardly the only artist to break down pianos (Raphael Montañez Ortiz's 1966 "Piano Destruction Concert" was a touchstone art event as well), her burning and drowning pianos attracted attention as much for their generative energy—the crackling of fire, the sound of rain invading a piano in the woods—as for their apparently destructive premise. In a broad sense, these works relate to the 1960s' smashing and burning of guitars onstage, but in a way that continues the process of decomposition over a longer period and in a new environment outside conventional concert venues.

Jacques Rancière has gone so far as to claim that "art can only be art when the question of whether it belongs to the art world or the 'real' world is unclear," in terms of what he calls its "sensory milieu."[22] Lockwood's *Piano Burning* and *Piano Drowning* exemplify this ambiguity not only in their physical placement outdoors but also in the variation in performance and audience framing. In each case, a simple set of instructions guides the performer to place an already "defunct" piano in a particular kind of outdoor setting, leave it, and either burn it or document its slow decay. Lockwood may have been influenced by earlier piano-drowning experiments in the Fluxus milieu, such as Mieko Shiomi's 1963 "Event for the Twilight," accompanied by handwritten instructions to "steep a piano in the water of a pool" and "play some piece of F. Liszt on the piano."[23] The Fluxus practice of writing musical scores with nonnotational graphics or in prose, describing the musicians' dress, gestures, and actions such as "scraping" the violin or "detuning" various instruments, likely influenced Lockwood as well. "In these rituals," writes Rui Eduardo Paes, "the most sacred postulates of erudite culture and the conventional concept of spectacle were systematically overthrown."[24]

All of this said, Lockwood did not set out primarily to "overthrow" cultural norms but rather to experiment with their materials in new settings. Her overall approach is one of "porousness" and attentive listening—not only to the materials in each composition but also to the surrounding cultural mood.[25] When she first burned a piano, in 1968 London, she was well aware that "we were burning American flags, political effigies, the status quo,"[26] and though she has never thought of herself as an activist, she "set out to capture the essence of immolation."[27] She found an abandoned upright piano in a dump, as households were casting them aside "to make room for television sets," moved it to an art festival site on the Thames, and, after inserting asbestos-wrapped microphones into the piano's case, added lighter fluid and set it aflame. A three-hour burning process left the instrument in embers and inspired Lockwood to hold an informal séance invoking the spirit of Beethoven.[28] This explicitly ritual aspect of the performance, in which the dead composer was asked what he thought of it, did not apparently yield a clear answer, except in a "strange affirmative blurp" on the burned-piano recording.[29]

As Lockwood further developed her practice around decomposing pianos, she combined renaturing with systematic documentation. Playing the piano in addition to photo-documenting it is an auditory and kinetic way to trace its overtaking by the elements, as it grows less in tune with the tempered scale but perhaps more in tune with its outdoor environment. This mixture of performance art and conventional instrumental playing creates an already multilayered intermedial complex. The addition of elemental media, as water meets the wood, copper, cast iron, and felt that make up the piano, carries the instrument into another, stranger perceptual experience. Textual scoring of the work brings it back into the realm of human culture in an oscillating relationship that keeps the nature/culture divide ambiguous. Lockwood's prose score for *Piano Drowning* (from 1972 in Amarillo, Texas) reads like this:

> Find a shallow pond with a clay/other hard bed in an isolated place.
> Slide upright piano into position vertically, just off-shore.
> Anchor the piano against storms, e.g. by rope to strong stakes.
> Take photographs and play it monthly, as it slowly sinks.
> *Note: All pianos used should already be beyond repair.*[30]

Lockwood's insistence on already defunct instruments raises questions about how "beyond repair" they actually are, whether from a musician's or observer's perspective; this caveat implies ethical responsibility toward economically and aesthetically prized instruments. With outdoor spaces as a stage, curiosity and even discomfort around the piano, as vulnerable as it is valuable, affirm Rancière's point about art working in liminal territory.

Lockwood's 1960s–70s piano works introduce another element beyond simply destroyed or decaying pianos in her metaphorical approach to instrument and body. The title *Piano Transplants,* initially inspired by heart transplants, works not only in the ambiguous space between life and art in Rancière's sense but also between object and body, human and plant, decomposition and salvage.[31] These works decompose pianos in a sense beyond violent destruction, as Lockwood was most interested in transitions between material states and their acoustic potentials—not just for the sake of disrupting musical tradition but also to discover something more about it. During her years of work with *Piano Transplants,* she also used a recording of a human heartbeat in her 1970 tape piece *Tiger Balm,* continuing to follow her interest in the body and with "sound as a conduit of connection with the nonhuman environment."[32]

A similar visual-art example from this period is Dennis Oppenheim's 1969 *Gallery Transplant,* in which the artist relocated gallery floor plans to a snowy stretch of gravel in Jersey City, New Jersey. Unlike this literal recontextualization, however, Lockwood's burning or drowning pianos rely on a more elusive, organic metaphor of transcorporeal organ replacement for the sake of survival. The question of what survives of a burned or decayed piano animates these works; from a contemporary ecological perspective, reembedding the piano's material in the natural world is a kind of composting, which leads to both literal and metaphorical renewal in a more-than-human world. In a more recent work that takes the opposite route to this nexus of death and regeneration, artist Selva Aparicio's "Time's Refrain" (2016–24) embeds wasps' nests inside an upright piano with its front panels removed, transplanting organic material *into* the instrument as in a surgical procedure.[33] The nests appear almost like internal organs inside the body of the piano, not unlike the placement of a snake's rattle inside a fiddle in Appalachian tradition, whether for luck or for the buzz.[34]

Such links between instruments and bodies became a point of discussion at the 2005 Ruined Piano Convergence, where Lockwood and others reflected on piano destruction not as an activist intervention but as a reflective and generative response to a screen-dominated age—well beyond the replacement of pianos by televisions in the 1960s. The conference notes put it this way: "If a concern with using noise or distortion for the production of music is, in some ways, a hangover from the modernist avant-garde, its transformation into a biological phenomenon during our digital age represents a distinctly novel development."[35] The term *biological* refers to the piano's resonant materiality, particularly in ruined pianos that can still be played or sounded by fire or wind or even insects, not as conventional music but as a combination of wood, metal, and textile that mediates sound waves outdoors. From the perspective of media archaeology (a field of study mostly focused on relations between present and past media technologies), long-decayed pianos could appear as fossils of an older, analog age, insistently remaining and echoing in a field or forest or pond. Music archaeology, a related field that investigates prehistoric instruments and culture, has informed contemporary artworks similar to Lockwood's—for example, Scottish artist Ruth Ewan's 2012 *The People's Instruments,* which included a ritual sacrifice of a burning piano in a lake, imitating ancient burial practices.[36] In this case, the piano becomes a stand-in for a body, enacting the "biological" shift at the metaphorical as well as material level.

Context in Music History: Expanding the Sounds of Music

Lockwood responded to the 1960s artistic climate as a composer as well as a material artist. The Fluxus movement that informed her work drew on innovations in several different media and genres, from Marcel Duchamp's readymades to composer John Cage's philosophy of sound, chance, and silence.[37] Just as ordinary objects became part of art exhibitions, materials not normally viewed as musical (such as stones, shells, coins, and glasses of water in Cage's 1952 *Water Music*) took on important roles in concert performance. Lockwood's early compositions experimented with glass as an acoustic medium, from "cullet (glass 'rocks' formed as waste products in the cooling process) to ultra-thin microglass from which electron microscopy slides are made," as a way to follow her own interest in timbre and the playful approach of Fluxus sound poets.[38] Whether working with glass or pianos, Lockwood is curious about resonances not organized according to scored music. In a collection of listening exercises that she compiled with her partner, Ruth Anderson, she applied the same decontextualizing approach to words: "Choose a word and repeat it until it loses its lexical meaning and becomes 'only' a sound."[39]

Unlike Cage's experiments with nonmusical objects in concert, Lockwood's *Piano Transplants* take the instrument outside the concert hall or living room. An indoor acoustic space, especially one shaped with wood, is still ecologically related,[40] but removing the piano from its normal habitat questions the conventions of art and music as culturally confined practices. In opening the body of the piano to wind, fire, water, plants, insects, and weather, Lockwood defamiliarizes it as an instrument and also, as Vadim Keylin has pointed out, treats it as a ready-made "sound sculpture" with aeolian potentials of passive sound.[41] This phenomenon, related to the movement of air over sand or other flexible surfaces, occurs most obviously when wind blows through harp strings, creating eerie overtones. With both composer and performer absent (except in some cases of experimentation and documentation), Lockwood's instruments also take on an acousmatic quality, as in some electronic music in which the sound's source is not clear. Instead, audiences hear "the air and water streams, making the listener aware of what is usually inaudible," while at the same time transforming the very environment in which an instrument is "consumed."[42] Thus the piano becomes a medium between artist and environment, culture and nature, music and noise.

Lockwood's particular interest in the piano followed a long trajectory of experiments with the instrument's materiality and sonic potentials even before the twentieth century. Before the grand piano was standardized for mass production in the 1880s, instrument builders tested a wide range of sizes, materials, and combinations "to alter the sound of the instrument, attaching frames, pedals, objects" and even "mandolin attachments."[43] Ancient instruments like the water-powered Alexandrian hydraulis may have influenced later curiosities such as the *pyrophone,* or "fire organ," invented by a French physicist in the mid-nineteenth century; this instrument used flames to generate vibration in glass pipes—perhaps a kind of "controlled burning" piano.[44] The practice of adding to or exposing the piano's resonating materials continued with work in the early 1900s by Henry Cowell exploiting the piano's strings, in what is called "inside" rather than "prepared" piano, which usually involves objects attached to the instrument while the pianist plays the keyboard.[45] John Cage's 1940s *Bacchanale* and *Sonatas and Interludes* are examples of prepared piano, with "very specific instructions" using screws and bolts to augment the piano's percussive qualities.[46] George Crumb's 1970s *Makrokosmos* combines both inside and prepared aspects of extended-technique performance, with amplification added to the instrument, as the pianist plucks and mutes the strings, plays the keyboard, and even cries out into the body of the piano. In the 1990s, artist Rebecca Horn's *Concert for Anarchy* went so far as to partially disassemble a grand piano and suspend it from the ceiling of an art gallery, splaying keys and hammers that would sound in "a clumsy and unpredictable cycle," upending visitors' received ideas of a piano's cultural function.[47]

Contemporary experimental piano works—many by female composers—often add electronic enhancements along with stones, fishing line, the pianist's voice, or "de-tuning" techniques.[48] Improvisational composer Magda Mayas describes the work of several female composers who have "dismantled" pianos to expose the strings and soundboard, as a radical response to the inviting challenge of a "massive, static, and immobile" instrument that she approaches as a kind of "Pandora's box."[49] This curiosity also drives Swedish composer Lisa Streich, who premiered her work *Orchestra of Black Butterflies* at the 2024 Venice Music Biennale; two motorized pianos "tuned a quartertone apart" and with paper strips on the strings create a "ghostly lyricism" and the "slightly woozy quality of a slowing-down music box."[50] At the 2024 Ultima contemporary music festival in Oslo, Zhanna Gladko's *Dancing into Fire* formed a sonic, sculptural, and gestural reaction to her father's own piano destruction work from 2015, with a circle of piano wires suspended onstage and sounded by female musicians and poets. This work critiques not only patriarchal inheritance but also political oppression of female artists in Belarus and Iran.[51] Its cultural resonance recalls violent uses of piano wire as instruments of execution by hanging, for example in the case of Hitler's would-be assassins in 1944 and in the

USSR as well,[52] making the reclaiming of the copper strings in a harmonious circle all the more striking. In the blurry zone between contemporary music and visual art, Naama Tsabar's 2024 *Estuaries,* part visual artwork, part composition, and part participatory experiment, invites museum visitors to play piano wires strung from felt panels or inside openings in the walls while circling pieces of broken guitars on the floor. The wires resonate throughout the space in random chords and dissonances, as various hands touch and release them. Occasional scored performances activate the deconstructed instruments as well.[53]

Making new sounds with familiar instruments, a common practice in contemporary art and music today, was only one aspect of mid-twentieth-century avant-garde piano composition. Cage's famous *4′33″* (1951/52) may be the best-known example, with the pianist instructed to sit at the instrument without playing at all, foregrounding random sounds in the concert hall instead of scored music. Salomé Voegelin has pointed out that however open-ended this work appears, it still treats silence as "a matter of musicology, a 'disciplined' and organized sound... and this music remains a Western, singular, hegemonic concept. Once ordered, silence loses its blurring relational potential and cannot create the criticality of proximity and fuzziness."[54] As a young composer, Annea Lockwood sought out this very "loosening of control" and finding "details blurred" through listening, particularly in her work with composer Morton Feldman: "Letting a resonance play out entirely before striking the next tone was a central teaching and it reinforced something the glass concert had taught me too—to give a sound time—let it 'live out its life' fully, listening closely to the whole energy/timbre change."[55] In Lockwood's own prepared piano work, *Earwalking Woman* (1996), the pianist focuses on listening to the instrument's strings and frame when stroked or struck, responding with improvisation.[56]

This receptive attitude is also important to the burning, drowning, or what Lockwood has called "permanently prepared piano."[57] These instruments take time to resonate, even before human hands touch them in their damaged states. Approaching a piano first from a listening rather than a performing position treats the instrument not as a tool for rendering a musical score but rather as a material, sounding object in its own right. The emancipation of the piano as an object is also evident in Lockwood's scoring of these works *after* burning or transplanting the instruments.[58] This apparently backward process permits an intimate curiosity that counters the tendency toward spectacle in twentieth-century art. Lockwood has observed that "while many of her peers in Fluxus and other artistic movements were offering 'piano destruction corridas' throughout the 1960s," she was less interested in "destruction" than in "something less predictable, arising from the gradual action of natural forces . . . on an instrument designed for maximum control."[59] In a 1991 composers' discussion for *EAR* magazine, Lockwood noted that she uses specific outdoor sites "as an acoustic part of the piece" and that one of her "slowly sinking" piano transplants is still partially playable twenty years after being placed in a Texas pond. "Classical music," the moderator (composer R. I. P. Hayman) responded, and Lockwood laughed, saying more than her words did about the project's implicit critique of Eurocentric and even anthropocentric musical objects.[60]

In the concert hall, audiences expect to hear certain forms of music, with the assumption that the instruments will function in tune. Thanks to the musicians and personnel behind the scenes, they usually do. At the same time, these instruments are sensitive objects, extremely responsive to changes in temperature and humidity. A grand piano in particular is so heavy, difficult to move, and complicated to tune that it requires physical labor and specialized expertise. From the perspective of conventional musical practice, deliberately exposing a piano to the elements equals destroying it as a musical instrument. What Lockwood points out, however, is that these pianos do not stop being sounding objects; the sounds they make are simply, and often radically, different. In a contemporary example, a spirit of curious experimentation informs Shohei Kudo's Instagram-friendly videos of a "nature-prepared" toy piano in a moving stream, perhaps inspired by Cage's (indoor) *Water Music* with stones and twigs inserted into the piano's gamelan-like structure. The resulting sound is playful, repetitive in improvisation with close intervals, and strangely soothing.[61] This project works in a similar way to the bite-size TikTok music theory demonstrations that younger musicians, less bound to concert traditions, are producing to make art music more approachable.

Whether online, in a museum, or outdoors, with Annea Lockwood's influence in the background, pianos are more often becoming objects for experimentation and play. Even a piano that no longer makes pitched tones is still a sounding object, as in Nikita Gale's "Stolen Time" at the 2024 Whitney Biennial, a work featuring a player piano that only sounds the "tuneless plonks of keys moving down and up" and making an uneasy "link" between music as "either a score or a physical performance."[62] The Canadian duo Decomposing Pianos has described their experiments with a century-old instrument, recording the piano after long exposure to rain and eventually removing the keys, until only the "iron harp" inside remains; they find that "the harp is a new voice from within the decomposing instrument."[63] A 2024 project by Simone Keller literally takes a piano apart, piece by piece, inviting a group of improvisers to make sounds with the instruments' separated parts and to take a soundwalk along the "hidden rivers" of Tbilisi, Georgia, accompanied by a toy piano.[64] This freeing of the instrument from its concert-hall associations and allowing it to sound even in pieces expands ideas of what is music and what is noise, and what is in and out of human control.

Composers who work with renatured and/or decomposing pianos show a range of willingness to let the instrument go. Especially because a piano is often described as a "string instrument under keyboard control" (as an organ is a wind instrument under keyboard control),[65] the idea of authoritative structure often carries over into artistic experiments. The open curiosity of the Canadian project, Keller's collective improvisation, and Kudo's toy water piano is not always in play. In the 1991 interview with Lockwood, composer Gordon Monahan explained his own 1988 *Aeolian Piano* work that took a different approach, with a helicopter airlifting the instrument to a hilltop overlooking the St. John's harbor in Newfoundland. In that case, extra 170-foot strings were attached from the sound board to the cliff face and then amplified, creating aeolian sheets of sound "that could be heard almost a kilometer away."[66] This grand work does respond to its environment, but it also colonizes it by drilling into a cliff face, rather than simply letting a piano break down into sounding matter in a particular ecosystem. Even Tori Wrånes's similar work *Loose Cannon* (2010), with a piano bolted to a cliff face in northern Norway and then set on fire, appears as a controlled, spectacular experiment.[67] Lockwood's interest in letting go of control of the instrument (not just preparing it to respond to the wind) creates a humbler, more receptive link to the surrounding land. In this way it connects to the practice of finding already ruined pianos and discovering how their remaining materiality sounds.

Ruined Pianos: Exposure to the Elements

As part of nineteenth-century colonizing efforts, seven hundred thousand pianos were shipped from Europe to Australia, where the instrument became (according to a French music critic who visited in the 1880s) "a necessary piece of furniture," however "cheap and nasty" in a "humble dwelling."[68] Many of these pianos were later abandoned to the elements, out in the bush on sheep station land, in a collapsed shed, or even in a ghost town's ruined bar, with wind and dust blowing in for decades. Campion's New Zealand–set film *The Piano* took some inspiration from this colonialist history, making the piano the protagonist. The piano emerges from a sea journey with the sounds of a perfectly in-tune recording, foregrounding the instrument's role as a stand-in for Eurocentric culture, in an inconsistency between audiovisual narrative and the piano's material condition. The instrument is clearly used in a metaphorical way to stage colonial cultural hegemony, as the sound of a piano in these films is both more stable and less frail than it should be. Thus the film makes an audiovisual argument that postcolonial novels tend to make, about art music and instruments as representatives of colonial power. This contrast also exposes the breakdown of colonializing projects involving musical instruments, which have become part of the landscape in places where they were meant to solidify Western cultural values. This phenomenon becomes palpable in a short story by Kerryn Goldsworthy about nineteenth-century Australia: "Perhaps all over this terrifying country there are Dead Pianos—left on beaches—abandoned on tracks—pushed over cliffs—rotting in ruined huts and cabins—making peculiar homes for birds and mice and spiders playing witches' music among the strings and fretwork, and the silk all gone to rags."[69]

A surprising number of these renatured pianos still make sound, and the practice of finding and improvising on them has become something of a cultural adventure. When composer and improviser Ross Bolleter discovered a ruined piano on a sheep station in 1987, he pulled and released the old strings as the "piano roared and groaned."[70] He had found a new mission. A century after the French critic's report, in 1991, Bolleter and extended-technique pianist Stephen Scott founded WARPS, the World Association for Ruined Piano Studies. Projects have included symposia, intentional piano transplants in locations across the world, an outdoor piano sanctuary in Australia, and improvisational as well as composed performances on the instruments. The organization has also developed an idiosyncratic taxonomy of broken and weathered pianos, with the following terminology, depending on where the instruments are found and in what condition:

—neglected (including veranda pianos),
—abandoned (including shed pianos),
—weathered,
—decayed,
—ruined,
—devastated,
—decomposed, and
—annihilated as after having been blown up by a landmine planted in it by the Germans retreating northwards through Italy in 1945.[71]

Bolleter's own text becomes rhapsodic when describing these renatured instruments, touching on the piano's cultural and colonialist freight:

> The only unchanging law is the law of change. Ruins are what remain. A piano judiciously left in the open and exposed to all weathers will ruin. All that fine nineteenth-century European craftsmanship, all the damp and unrequited loves of Schumann, Brahms and Chopin dry out, and degrade to a heap of rotten wood and rusting wire. The piano returns to aboriginality, goes back to the earth. Plucking the bass strings on an ancient weathered piano whose sound board is cracked wide open can produce astonishing pitch bends, then cataclysmic shuddering. Sounds which would be suppressed in conventional performance are given full rein. When those arch symbols of European musical culture and cultural imperialism linger as Ruined Pianos, they sing of transience, failure and loss. They sing of all that we loved that will never come again—the loss of home, the fading away of prestige and glory. They sing the chaos at the heart of the colonial enterprise, an Australian expression of the heart of darkness—the dark heart howling its cracked anthems.[72]

In a description of ruined piano playing techniques, Bolleter is more practical, providing instructions on how to play while sitting on the ground or with hands upside-down, how to force down sustain pedals with erasers, how to work the hammers when the keys no longer sound, and how to use already broken-off pieces of the piano "to strike or stroke the strings."[73] A 2021 documentary shows Bolleter improvising on various ruined pianos, showing what wild sounds (also perhaps in the metaphorical sense of rewilding instruments) can an emerge when a keyboard no longer registers the diatonic, tempered scale that forms the spine of European classical music. Like Annea Lockwood outlining her piece *Earwalking Woman,* Bolleter puts listening first, to find out what "metallic percussive effects, . . . squeaks, squawks, and grinding sounds" the instrument will yield.[74] This approach reverses conventional musical training, with "forms of musical creation emerging from the very fabric of the sounding material, rather than from the abstraction of the written score."[75] At the same time, Bolleter hears each piano's haunting by past music played from score, "the voice of the past in it."[76]

Surprisingly in this documentary (as well as in Sophy Roberts's history-travelogue *The Lost Pianos of Siberia*), ruined pianos elicit little commentary on the ecological implications of instruments decaying in the hinterlands, in terms of varnish or other chemical remnants, structural shelter for nonhuman creatures, or broader questions of human materials left to rot outdoors. Likewise, a 2022 conference on Lockwood's work raised further awareness of her site-based sound work, with papers on topics such as "sonic agencies" and "material experience[s] of time"—but less attention than might be expected to the climate and cultural implications of a piano's dramatic demise.[77] Still, although Bolleter's ruined-piano works do not respond explicitly to climate or biodiversity crisis like much environmental art and music today, they do invite multispecies listening. Bolleter's written reflection on the Ruined Piano Sanctuary does include some observations about nonhuman sharers in the instrument's materiality: "a nineteenth century British Challen piano engulfed by white ants that have transformed its insides into a gothic cathedral of ingested wood," a rats' nest in the top of a British upright, and a German piano left in a dam and "occupied by frogs." At night, apparently, "you can hear them jumping about on the strings creating strange and subtle accompaniments to their croaking."[78]

In a similar nod toward multispecies receptivity, Lockwood has recently commented on her wish not to "listen *to* something" but rather to "listen with the neighborhood."[79] Her decaying instruments in *Piano Drowning* and *Piano Garden* certainly invite other creatures to nest, feed, sleep, chirp, croak, or simply pass through. Like composer Harrison Birtwistle's 2012 *Moth Requiem* for choir, alto flute, and three harps, inspired by a poem about a moth caught in a piano and making "unearthly noises,"[80] openness to otherness in a human-made instrument may foster more multispecies awareness than a didactic work of art would do. Interestingly, all these works echo older folk-music traditions, such as the placement of snake rattles in Appalachian fiddles. This practice makes a buzzing sound that warns against playing the strings too hard, adds mojo to the music, and perhaps even drives the devil away.[81] The ritual aspect of burning or drowning pianos may be implicit in most cases, but it does recall folk practices of bonfires, plant offerings, and music as magic or medicine. Invading a piano with fire or water, elements now associated with climate crisis, can work homeopathically (in the sense of poison as medicine) in facing the source of grief after wildfires or hurricanes.

Environmental Art and Performance

For all of Lockwood's focus on sound and metaphorical "transplants," her works also fall within a larger tendency toward ecological art in the 1960s and 1970s. From the broad perspective of transplanting art outside, *Piano Transplants* relate to the era's large-scale land art innovations, usually created by male artists, including Dennis Oppenheim's *Annual Rings* (1968) and Robert Smithson's *Spiral Jetty* (1970). Though these artists generally worked by manipulating aspects of the land itself, they saw site-specific works as ways to bring art outside the museum, just as Lockwood was moving pianos from the concert hall or living room. That said, as in the case of Gordon Monahan's cliff piano as spectacle, these works do not show the entangled, listening approach of Lockwood's outdoor works; nor do they indicate attunement to pressing ecological concerns. Although Rachel Carson's groundbreaking and disturbing book *Silent Spring* (1962) was very much in the public consciousness, with the first Earth Day celebrated in 1970, it took time for artists to move from using "earth as material," as in the Spiral Jetty, toward the direct ecological messaging of Joseph Beuys's *7000 Oaks* (shown at the documenta 7 contemporary art exhibition) and Agnes Denes's *Wheatfield—A Confrontation* in lower Manhattan, both projects appearing in 1982.[82] These works not only used soil and plants as material but also signaled humankind's destructive relationship to nature.

In the late 1960s and early 1970s, concerns about air pollution, nonrecyclable waste, and harmful pesticides were prevalent, and the image of a decaying piano likely took on connotations beyond Lockwood's original transplant idea. Though her scores are not intended as ecocriticism, their ritual earthiness may indicate why the piano burnings and transplants are reperformed, revisited, and rewatched today—and why they have inspired numerous later explorations of pianos burning or decaying outdoors. From the perspective of environmental art history, which studies past artworks with attention to the ecological conditions of their time as well as their implications in the current climate crisis,[83] any act of renaturing and/or decomposing a piano takes on new significance. A 2025 performance on a piano left to decay for five months in Copenhagen's Cisterns underground art space is one of many works building on Lockwood's legacy, not only creating a "sonic sculpture where all sonic ideals collapse"[84] but also pointing to moisture, mold, and the threat of future flooding in low-lying Denmark.

Through ongoing iterations in slow films and art performances, burning or decaying pianos invite associations with today's monster fires and floods, in addition to questions about the instrument's extractivist history and role as a kind of cultural sacrifice. Today, when musicians and dancers perform with melting glaciers, artists create installations foregrounding waste and decay, composers write music about and for a heating planet, and "vegetal theatre" entangles human culture in nonhuman settings,[85] Lockwood's 1960s and 1970s piano performances seem to be decades ahead of their time. The "durational" aspect of Ólafur Elíasson's well-known *Ice Watch,* in which blocks of ice melted as a "nonhuman presence in a dense human space" in Paris in 2015, or of Jason deCaires Taylor's underwater sculptures "colonized" and decayed by the ocean environment,[86] pick up the thread of Lockwood's decomposing, renatured pianos, with more direct environmental messaging. Some piano-related works of the past decade respond explicitly to environmental crisis and its human costs, as in a 2017–18 installation by Ryuichi Sakamoto and Shiro Takatani, *Is Your Time.* This work creates a meditation on the 2011 earthquake and tsunami in Japan, with an abandoned piano augmented electronically to play as if by itself, "voicing" the presence of its unknown, former owners, sometimes with "broken keys."[87] All of these works make human and nonhuman losses (past or future) physically perceptible, especially in the case of *Ice Watch,* in which visitors can touch and press their ears to what feels like a piece of melting glacier.

Recent scholarship on art and the Anthropocene shows a preoccupation with death, extinction, and haunting—not only as a ghostly trace of human presence but also as a possibility of new, strange compostings and coalescences. Jill H. Casid coined the term *Necrocene* to indicate the fallout from human pillaging of earthly resources: "In representing the Anthropocene as a scene of genocide precipitated by the fatal transformation of the world into orbis, or territorialized globe, by techniques of colonial landscaping . . . it might, rather, be named the Necrocene."[88] Still, although empire is sown as invasive seeds, Casid argues, "such ostensibly founding scenes of dissemination as devices of bio- and necropower set the stage for other possibilities, for there is arguably nothing predictable about the effects of transplantation, production, and reproduction or the kinds of composting and decay that turn what I term *death-in-life* into emergent forms."[89] Casid's use of the term *transplant* is hopeful in the sense of Lockwood's metaphorical idea; something of a decomposed instrument survives and challenges humans to reimagine what music, sonic materiality, and listening can be. The results are usually surprising. As Nils Bubant writes, "Anthropocene landscapes of death and extinction are . . . also inhabited by emergent and unexpected constellations of life, nonlife, and afterlife."[90] Perhaps Bolleter's observations about frogs, ants, and rats invading ruined pianos has more relevance than simply novelty. The piano's afterlife is not only a haunting through decay but also an invitation toward ecological attunement through what was once a domesticated instrument.

Annea Lockwood's instruction to photograph and play a *Piano Transplant* monthly is one way of documenting environmental art history. This is not just a history of death through decay but also a tracing of microclimates and monthly cycles of light, darkness, rain, cold, heat, humidity, or drought. Each time the piano is played, its tuning is more chaotic, its parts and pieces looser (as keyboard control breaks down), its crevices more crowded with nonhuman occupants. This very looseness can become an opportunity for wild, percussive sound, as in Ross Bolleter's improvisations on a ruined piano. In the case of a burned piano, the instrument's frame reveals its inner harp, becoming ambiguous in the traditional taxonomy of music-making, before it falls to the ground in a thrumming, sparking mass. If the instrument is eventually split into firewood, as in the Christmas Eve scene in *Billy Elliot,* it signifies human survival of the implicitly animal kind, breaking down the old, false nature/culture divide for the sake of winter warmth. In a time of undeniable global heating, a burned piano signals loss from wildfire, too, and perhaps a sacrificial offering of human cultural ambitions, never without planetary cost.

This chapter has linked histories of decomposing instruments to show the complexity of potential meanings in works like Annea Lockwood's *Piano Transplants* or Ross Bolleter's improvisations on ruined pianos. From military histories of burning pianos to postcolonialist neglect of instruments in the Australian bush, and from Fluxus nonperformances to "prepared," "inside," or literally deconstructed piano works, the instrument has invited a wide range of material experiments. From an environmental art history perspective, pianos relocated outdoors, as well as pianos burned in an artistic ritual, carry more significance amid current ecological concerns than they may have fifty years ago. Decomposing a piano—subjecting it to fire, water, weather, plant growth, and nonhuman creatures—ultimately reembeds it in the world from which its materials came.

2 PIANO AS MEDIUM, MATERIAL, AND REPRESENTATION

IN CHAPTER 1, WE BEGAN WITH examples of decomposed pianos in popular culture and art history, from Europe and the United States to Australia and Japan. Why this instrument, among so many? Is the piano unique in its size, complexity (as a hybrid string and percussion instrument), and control (with up to thirty thousand pounds of pressure on the strings)? Is its freighted colonialist history a force not only to be reckoned with but also to be broken down? Is it so far removed from its origins in forest and mineral deposits that it has become "disembedded" from nature and into the concert hall?[1] In this sense, however "embodied" the experience of classical performance,[2] the piano is quite unlike the wooden Japanese *shō* mouth organ,[3] for example, which the musician tunes to her own body, to the audience, to the performance space, and to the natural world outside. Does the piano hold special capacities for experimentation and listening when it loses its function as a performance instrument?

These questions touch on the piano's material complexity, its function as a musical medium, and its historical and cultural resonances. As Aaron S. Allen has put it in his approach to "ecoörganology," "More than just tools . . . musical instruments are also objects and symbols of fascination, investment, contemplation, worship, and desire: they even have social lives, as if they were subjects and not just objects."[4] Now, in this chapter, we explore how unconventional treatments of the piano call attention to its materiality, communicative potential, and representation of social power structures. We approach the piano not only as an instrument that channels the sounds of particular cultural moments but also from an intermedial perspective. As we introduce intermedial theory and connect it with "elemental" and "radical" media approaches, these combined frameworks help us to understand the piano as a medium in its own right. Underlying our theoretical discussion, the piano's physical properties of wood, copper, iron, leather, and felt, as well as its situated sounds, make the instrument a complex medium for meaning-making.

After providing some background on the piano's history and cultural enshrinement in circles of European privilege, we build on feminist and postcolonialist critiques of musical performance as a tool of social power, materially represented in the piano. Musical instruments thus not only represent and mediate music as aesthetically pleasing sounds but also may imply uses of music to dominate and control. Because of these representations and cultural affordances, music's physical force can be co-opted as an agent of oppressive systems; the material origins of many musical instruments (rosewood or ivory, for example) have been blatantly extractivist; the piano's history is wounding in whom it leaves out. At the same time, resisting the temptation to throw out the art-music baby with its problematic bathwater, we show that music itself is not a tainted or toxic phenomenon. The effects of sound remain too multifaceted for easy binaries. In this chapter, we do not set out to trace a complete postcolonial history of the instrument but to highlight the historical movement of the piano itself in colonialist contexts, making the familiar object in a Western living room or concert hall appear strange in different settings. Similar defamiliarization occurs in the piano's movement into more-than-human ecosystems, a move that chapter 3 explores with posthumanist perspectives on renatured and decomposed pianos.

The Piano as Medium: Intermedial Perspectives

Physical, material, and symbolic perceptions are all in play when we approach the piano as a medium. When we speak of media here, we are not thinking simply of material objects or devices, such as books, computers, or musical instruments, as tools of communication. Instead, we consider the material underpinning of all human communication. The term *media,* from the Latin word for "in between," refers to the interplay of material objects, human perceptions, and semiotic processes, as they enable communication across time and space. This complex mesh of mediation unfolds in multiple dimensions. For instance, like other tools of physical action and perception, musical instruments can be said to extend human perception. Instruments make pressure waves perceptible, mediating human awareness of the larger world.[5] But we do not perceive musical instruments primarily as physical tools that transform air pressure deviations into sound. They are also objects designed to produce organized sound waves that we hear and interpret within an aesthetic framework. All sounds produced on a piano (even when handled by a beginner or nonmusician) are already qualified and evaluated within musical conventions.

To approach a piano's meaning potential beyond conventional sounds and musical contexts, we draw on intermedial theory. This field of study has developed in the humanities to approach art forms as media in their own right. An intermedial perspective explores relationships within and between media by tracing the relationships among objects, perceptions, semiosis, and conventions[6] and is specifically useful in exploring phenomena that challenge the conventional boundaries of media and communication.[7] This perspective enables us to trace shifts in perception that occur when musical instruments are displaced and/or decomposed. Works like Annea Lockwood's *Piano Transplants* force us to reassess our received understanding of what a piano means—specifically, what kind of meaning it conveys when its primary task, to produce musical sounds, is challenged.

Intermedial analyses tend to explore how media and materials shape works of art and draw attention to unexpected, unnoticed, or underlying meaning potentials; this is a useful perspective if we want to tease out the unconventional use of musical instruments. To approach this interplay of matter, perception, and semiosis, Lars Elleström proposes a conceptual framework of media types and media modalities that applies to all kind of media products, although in different ways. Our perception of distinctive media types, Elleström stresses, is based on interaction with specific media products—songs and other musical pieces, or social media posts and comments.[8] When engaging with media products, we interact with material objects (of physical phenomena) as technical media of display. Technical media of display such as books, canvases, or digital screens offer interfaces for us to perceive basic media types or communicative resources that we use in many contexts, such as texts, images, gestures, or sounds. Depending on context and convention, we recognize and evaluate these basic media types as belonging to qualified media types. Thus, we identify a text as belonging to "literature" or "journalism" and recognize a specific image as an "oil painting" or a "caricature."[9] With Elleström's concepts, we can show that what we call music relies on the interplay of bodies and objects manipulating pressure waves as a technical medium, which in turn enables us to perceive the basic media type of organized sounds. Again, depending on context and convention, we categorize these organized sounds as "classical music," "techno," or "commercial jingle." However, when listeners are unfamiliar with these conventions or fail to perceive patterns of organization, they might only hear sounds or noise.

To analyze the entanglements of media and meaning within a media product, Elleström proposes the following modalities: material, spatiotemporal, sensorial, and semiotic.[10] This framework is useful in understanding the web of situated objects, their perception, and the semiosis that takes place in any musical performance. In this study, we use it to trace what happens when musical instruments are treated in a way *not* meant primarily to produce musical sounds, thus activating other forms of meaning-making. Moving the piano out of its conventional indoor habitat and not using it to produce music draws attention to the object in itself, which mediates more than expected musical sounds. Elleström's framework will allow us (in more detail in chapter 4) to address material, sensorial, spatiotemporal, and semiotic aspects separately before pointing out their interactions. This approach shows that even if no music is performed on a decomposing instrument, we still can engage with these objects in meaningful ways.

At the same time, the process raises new questions. How do audiences used to conventional performance practice make sense of piano decomposition if it radically questions and possibly transforms previous experiences? Why are these experiences—from Annea Lockwood's experiments to today's richly varied offshoots—so compelling? When we ask how the piano functions as a medium beyond being a musical instrument, it also moves beyond the three media types that Elleström delineates. In unconventional uses, the piano is no longer primarily perceived as a technical device to produce organized sounds, qualified according to or in dialogue with musical conventions. The object shifts into a strange place, with sounds distorted in ways that we cannot describe according to genre; we react to material situatedness and sensorial perception rather than to a "musical" experience.

Elleström's framework has already shown how mediation through material and physical phenomena is fundamental to communication. Strictly speaking, there is no such thing as unmediated communication,[11] although the objects, bodies, technologies, and resources involved will vary in different contexts. However, approaching decomposing pianos, and thinking of a piano as a medium, requires a more elemental (or radical) way to approach mediation that does not directly actualize communicative conventions. This approach would need to move from a specific message to an experience of relations, and from the perception of the musical instrument as a sounding tool to a material body performing more-than-musical patterns. Media convey conventionally coded content, but they are also able to do this because they are modes of contact with the environment. They *perform* relatedness.

In our approach to decomposing pianos and renatured instruments, we draw not only on intermedial theory but also on theories of radical and elemental media to describe how these materials operate. Burning and drowning pianos push beyond the boundaries of interhuman communication and cultural messages; they raise questions of entanglement between human and nonhuman, or between media and environment. Media theorists Richard Grusin and John Durham Peters have explored mediation not only as a part of communication but also as a relational force, not simply delivering a message and offering content but providing connection at a more fundamental level. Richard Grusin derives the term *radical mediation* from the philosopher William James's concept of radical empiricism, which describes forms of world perception as "experienced relations."[12] Grusin applies this concept to the understanding of media, in that "mediation operates not just across communication, representation, or the arts, but is a fundamental process of human and nonhuman existence."[13] This idea of "radical mediation" does not primarily focus on the relation between media and the messages that are conveyed, but rather on how they create connectedness, how they "function technically, bodily, and materially to generate and modulate individual and collective affective moods or structures of feeling among assemblages of humans and nonhumans."[14]

Grusin's mention of "human and nonhuman" twice on one page indicates a shift toward the posthumanist perspective that informs our project as well. His emphasis on materiality and affect relates to notions of immediacy, as a sense of direct involvement in mediated content (when we forget about the medium and engage with the story world), or as a rhapsodic human experience of "Nature" (as in the Romantic period in literature). Grusin's radical media approach helps us to trace the physical interrelationships that might be perceived as "immediate." Human and nonhuman bodies ("fundamentally media" themselves) experience the in-between of mediation with all their senses.[15] At the same time, Grusin argues that mediation should not be seen as a fixed in-between position but instead as a more fundamental process that, by connecting actors, objects, and events, "generates or provides the conditions for the emergence of subjects and objects."[16] The intermediality field has begun to apply similar thinking, moving from meaning-making as human interpretation of signs to acknowledging the distributed agencies of more-than-human networks. This approach shows how animals and plants also function in sensory-cognitive systems to experience meaning as "embodied, embedded, enacted, and even extended beyond the (human) body."[17]

These more foundational aspects of mediation are useful in our exploration of what happens in the renaturing and decomposing of pianos, asking less what kind of message a burning piano communicates but rather which aspects of mediation are at work in the process. In an even more ecologically focused approach, John Durham Peters goes so far as to call water, air, fire, and earth "elemental media," or environmental phenomena (not objects and institutions) as media. Peters considers media as "infrastructures of being, the habitats and materials through which we act and are."[18] In his approach to digital and elemental networks, Peters moves away from "the urgency of the message to the nature of media (and media of nature)."[19] While the concept of elemental media aids in understanding the radical shifts of digital transformation (like Grusin, Peters points toward the metaphors of digital media, such as "networks" and "clouds" marking media as environment[20]), our focus here is on mediation beyond social, communicative conventions and toward human-nonhuman networks shaped by environmental forces.

Earth, water, air, and fire, Peters points out, provide environments for living beings; at the same time, humans design tools to domesticate the elements, from ships that navigate the oceans to aircraft that ply the air. But humans also use elements as media of communication and connection. Peters lists telling examples from the language of technology that still connect mass media and modern devices with the elemental forces of heat and light; for instance, "the German term for broadcasting, *Rundfunk,* contains the term *Funk* (spark) in tribute to the early history of radio, with its spark gap transmitters," or the Samsung "Galaxy Blaze" and "Ignite."[21] Along with Peters, Melody Jue has explored the meaning-making potentials of the ocean in *Wild Blue Media,* which includes chapters on inscription, data, and archival thinking—in the "residue of past marine life, sedimented" in limestone, for example.[22] In the emerging links between posthumanism and intermediality, Asun López-Varela Azcárate has described a "semiotic continuum between nature and culture" not dependent only on human cognition, a spectrum in which "materiality is punctured with meanings, becoming storied matter."[23]

An example from human-material semiotics that relates to our study of pianos is Peters's treatment of bells as markers of time and space. Bells are objects designed to use metal, air, and sound waves as media for communication. They not only communicate specific messages but in a more general way mobilize bodies and their physical capacity to affect their surroundings. Bells have been central to humans' sense of time passing and of rootedness in a specific place, connecting humans in fundamental ways with the elements. Peters points out that historically, bronze bells not only announced bad weather but were also credited with the power to change it, taking on uncanny, almost human attributes.[24] Bells thus work as a medium "both in signs and ontology," especially if one considers that the air has not always appeared "empty and open" but "was once possessed with spirits and pestilences."[25] Though Peters does not specifically link the bell's sounding metal with musical instruments, its structural function does have this in common with a piano's cast-iron frame. The bell's shape is as iconic as that of a grand piano too. And like a bell's associative links with hours of the day, worship services, picturesque tourist towns, weddings, funerals, or weather warnings, the piano's resonance calls up its own range of meanings, from concert halls to cartoon saloons, from Jane Austen novels to classic jazz, from street pianos to stadium pop.

The concept of elemental media provides an entry point for thinking about a piano as a complex medium, from the physical impact of its materiality to the organized sounds of music and the connotations it carries. This approach exposes the materials and forces at work in the instrument, however it is used. Stefan Östersjö has noted that violins and guitars are made out of wood and thus "used to be trees: they germinated from seeds, photosynthesised, grew, and most likely reproduced themselves; there are probably trees still growing in the world that are the offspring of these instruments."[26] Of course this is true of pianos as well. At the same time, Östersjö points out that musical instruments are not only tools made of a certain material, and thus "the sociomateriality of a musical instrument is arguably far more fine-grained than that of a hammer."[27] A toolbox's hammer is designed to hit nails on the head. The wooden hammers inside a piano are part of an entire system of pressure and release, with the aim to produce a specific sound. This particular use does not make the piano's hammers any less elemental or embodied, however. Alexandra Huang-Kokina has described the modern piano as "entail[ing] the most elaborate and diverse range of tactility in producing musical sound," as the pianist's upper-body movement extended through the fingers activates both percussive and string mechanisms that in turn release the piano's affective resonance.[28] The choice of tonewood, the tension in the copper wires, and the stiffness or softness of the hammers' action create an instrument-specific personality that pianists bring to life.

Material History of the Piano

After considering the intermedial and elemental relations between instruments and environments, we now address the piano's material-cultural implications. Apart from musical sounds, the piano as an object thus transmediates the instrument's cultural history. We now show why this instrument—mingled with the history of humans as "storied beings"[29]—incites strong reactions if burned or left to decay in nature.

With the elemental media involved in a piano's construction in mind, we also take into account the narrative dimension of material ecocriticism, in which, as Serenella Iovino and Serpil Oppermann have phrased it, "material forms—bodies, things, elements, toxic substances, chemicals, organic and inorganic matter, landscapes, and biological entitles—intra-act with each other and with the human dimension, producing configurations of meanings and discourses that we can interpret as stories."[30]

As a technical device that produces musical sounds, the piano carries a long and complicated history. The varied and overlapping stories of the piano's development would require a separate volume, but those stories' material dimension is important to our project. We consider the physical aspect of shifting tuning practices, an interplay that stretches across material and sensorial media modalities, to point out how decaying pianos still sound, even as their tuning breaks down. Pianos left outdoors expose the always looming problem of out-of-tuneness in an instrument that normally requires technical expertise to be performance ready. While the out-of-tune piano has become a trope in films, usually indicating nostalgia for a lost, past life (the baby grand associated with childhood and dreams in both the 1982 and 2017 *Blade Runner* films, for example), it is a very real threat to performers who depend on exact tuning when using different concert instruments each time they appear in public. Tuning an antique instrument highlights the paradoxical delicacy and tension within the massive body of a grand piano. An old, fragile instrument's internal string pressure may not be able to bear the tension of the standard 440 Hz tuning (for the A above middle C)—a problem solved by tuning the instrument slightly flat (with the wires slightly looser than they would be at 440 Hz).

The piano's precursor, the Baroque harpsichord (with many variants of its own), descended from the medieval stringed psaltery. On the material level, the harpsichord functions with a plucking mechanism rather than the hammers that attack the strings in the nineteenth-century pianoforte and the pianos of today. This means that the harpsichordist cannot vary the volume of each note, as a pianist can with differences in pressure. A harpsichord's close-fitted system of plectra (once made from bird quill and later from leather and eventually plastic), which pluck sets of several strings or "choirs," is as delicate as it is complex.[31] These vibrating strings create a beating effect, the chime-like timbre of the instrument, in addition to producing a pitch for each key. A second, upper manual (keyboard) in some instruments allows for slight differences in dynamics; in some cases, a lute stop creates a softer sound. The tensile strings need to be tuned often, as they are thinner and less pressurized than piano wires. Harpsichords are also much more sensitive to changes in temperature and humidity than pianos are. Long storage or lack of care can result in strings becoming so loose that the plectra cannot engage them at all, or some strings will sound (or not) depending on the day. As a result, the sound of a harpsichord is more mechanical but at the same time more delicate than that of a modern piano.

Based on its structural options (and thus moving from the material to the sensorial aspects of the instrument), the harpsichord became a testing ground for seventeenth- and eighteenth-century tonal experiments that radically changed how musical scales sound today. Unlike string instruments that can easily be retuned, or wind instruments already tuned to a particular key, a keyboard instrument relies on a whole system of tuning across the stepwise diatonic scale. The Western harmonic system most familiar today builds on the invention of tempered tuning in the 1600s. This tuning, with many variants of its own that are beyond this chapter's scope, solved some of the problems that resulted from the Pythagorean system of overtone-based intervals. This system lines up in a series of ratios that can be replicated by dividing a string at certain points, with unison as 1:1, octave as 2:1, and perfect fifth as 3:2. Though commonly combined in European harmony to create consonant chords, these intervals are not necessarily used in musical cultures based on pentatonic or microtonal tuning systems. Strangely, the overtone series of ratios only lines up to a point (the end of the scalar progression, where the sonic relationship begins to sound off). Thus, the semitones F-sharp and G-sharp, for example, are at very close but different frequencies, and as a result it is not possible to modulate between different keys without sounding out of tune. Tempered tuning, on the other hand, distributes this difference over all the semitones of a scale (with "well" and "equal" variations of its own). In this way, discrepancies between semitones that are close in natural tuning are imperceptibly balanced out. F-sharp and G-flat coincide on keyboard instruments in tempered tuning, a so-called enharmonic confusion that allows movement between different keys.

The spacious intervals of Pythagorean tuning were once heard as links in a network of micro- and macrocosmos, carrying "music of the spheres" connotations long after their enshrinement in ancient Greece. While these intervals sound strange to most listeners today, tightening their tonal distances seemed transgressive to musical conservatives of the 1600s.[32] Bach, however, appears to have relished this problem-solving effort and the invention of technologies to support it. Preludes in his *Well-Tempered Clavier* (1722, 1742) move through harmonic passages that must have sounded both dissonant and revelatory at the time; a pianist playing this music can easily imagine Bach's exploratory pleasure in moving to another key without the instrument itself sounding out of tune, for all the ear's adjustment to new intervallic distances. The temperament of most European classical music sounds completely predictable to ears accustomed to it now. The smooth transition between different keys and scales is one of the piano's characteristics that many pianists may take for granted. At the same time, this tuning was an act of disembedding the instrument from "natural" overtones and further removing it from sounds that would occur without human intervention. In Lars Elleström's model, the technical medium of keyboard instruments took on new, qualifying characteristics as changes to the tuning system yielded new cultural potentials. Thus, instruments like the piano became indicators for a controlled yet flexible sound.

Even after the period of tonal innovation, the move from harpsichord to fortepiano in the late eighteenth century was hardly straightforward, with many experiments with the body of the instrument: extra pedals to create drone effects, extra keys for sounding microtones, or even attachments of other instruments such as the mandolin.[33] Even the terms *fortepiano* and *pianoforte* did not apply in a clear trajectory, though the latter was more commonly used in the nineteenth century. During the early transitional period, differences in the heft or lightness of the instruments' hammer mechanisms depended on the English or Viennese schools of piano making. These variances partially determined the sound of music composed on the instruments at the turn of the century, including Mozart's delicate melodies and Beethoven's more full-bodied chords and scalar explorations.[34]

A modern piano's wooden case encloses a complex system of chain reactions. When the pianist strikes the keys, they function as levers, transferring that motive force to wooden hammers that in turn strike copper wires supported and kept in tension by a cast-iron metal frame, known as the harp.[35] Unlike a harpsichord, the piano's keyboard responds to varying finger pressure to move from soft to loud (piano to forte). Pedals further manipulate the piano's expressivity, both in terms of sustaining sound from one note to the next (also unlike the harpsichord, which requires more complicated fingering to connect notes in a phrase) and in dampening the whole keyboard to create a quieter effect mechanically. In its overall structure, the body of a piano is a system of regulation, as it mediates and moderates a wide range of pressure waves. Its soundboard, usually made of spruce, absorbs higher overtones as it carries vibrations from the struck strings. The cast-iron plate that floats over the soundboard keeps the whole system of high-tension copper wires from imploding; the matching system of delicately weighted wooden hammers rests on felt pads, working as a shock absorber in tandem with supportive leather knuckles.[36]

The process of making such a complex instrument is environmentally costly, not only in the extraction of wood and metal but also in the process of casting iron, which requires protective gear to avoid respiratory and nervous system effects from lead, manganese, and a long list of other air pollutants.[37] The practice of making keys from ivory (until the 1940s) gives the instrument an even more problematic history in colonialist and extractivist terms. Decomposing a piano is not simply the act of returning its wood and metal to their earthly sources; it also raises questions of how its processes of construction, and even the chemicals in its varnish, reveal the impossibility of human–nonhuman interaction without environmental cost.

Cultural History and Representation

The nineteenth-century European pianoforte marked a social—and spatial—transition from aristocratic and church performance culture to broader musical experience, mirroring the wider spectrum of tones the instrument could convey. The plucked harpsichord of courtly entertainment and operatic recitative had often played a supportive role as an improvised continuo instrument outlining harmonic frameworks, along with a cello. The more muscular, dynamically varied, and soloistic pianoforte could shine in its own right and not just as a chamber instrument. In one view, the nineteenth-century instrument "evolved" to meet the requirements of larger, more democratic concert halls, with the wires' tension increasing tenfold as a result of the addition of metal frames and a sound that would have seemed "thunderous" compared to the harpsichord.[38] In fact, this new instrument could respond to larger *or* smaller physical spaces, both concert halls and living rooms, evoking a full-scale orchestra, as in the showpieces of Franz Liszt or a miniature opera in three pages, as in Franz Schubert's intimately dramatic songs. European bourgeois families with a piano at home could host a *Liederabend,* practice amateur chamber music, or try out the latest piano reduction of an opera score. Solo improvisation (the core of Chopin's compositional method) became part of musical evenings in European salon culture as well. The piano became a medium for adapting larger forms of music into intimate form and for individualistic "genius" culture to develop around the instrument, as in the case of Liszt especially. As Lawrence Kramer has pointed out, the "visual excess" of Liszt's performativity—and the "pianomania" it fostered—risked obscuring the sound of the music itself, but it contributed to the "dynamics of modern mass entertainment" associated with grand pianos today.[39]

For all its uses as a showcase for male performativity, the nineteenth-century pianoforte was also strongly associated with domestic femininity, taking on additional qualifying characteristics. Female composers like Fanny Mendelssohn and Clara Schumann produced vital piano works of their own, but without the recognition their male counterparts received. For most young women, the piano represented a certain type of middle-class femininity, a suitable occupation for wives and daughters that provided both discipline and diversion and guaranteed a more modest body position than when playing the flute (traditionally considered unbecoming for young women playing with moist, pursed lips) or the cello (with legs spread out).[40] With its central role in the education of girls, the piano provided discipline to the female body and signaled both "the family's wealth and the daughter's virtue."[41] Families from the middle into the upper classes could also show off their accomplished daughters in the heteronormative marriage market so vividly described in Jane Austen's novels—though actual pianistic accomplishment was less important than the act of appearing at the keyboard for the male gaze.[42] A key scene in Austen's novel *Persuasion* illustrates how playing the piano kept women physically in place: Captain Wentworth moves freely through the room during Anne's performance, while she is, as Gillian Dooley notes, "hemmed in both physically and by social convention."[43]

Thus, beyond its functions as a musical and social instrument, the pianoforte became a (conventional) symbol of male genius in the concert hall and of well-bred femininity in the domestic sphere. Whether in upper- or middle-class nineteenth-century homes, the piano took on almost transcendent overtones. As pianist Arthur Loesser notes in his history of the instrument, "the possession of a keyboard instrument had become such a habit among those who could afford it that it ceased to be an object of simple ostentation; the habit had become sanctified,"[44] taking an idea from a religious to a cultural context. This sanctification came with colonialist and ecological costs—not only in the production of pianos from materials harvested in South America and Africa but also in the broad effort at cultural erasure of Indigenous peoples during nineteenth-century expansion in North America. Many nineteenth-century pioneers moving West in covered wagons brought a piano with them, carrying music as a sign of cultural legitimacy even in the most hardscrabble desert towns. Hymns and sentimental songs drowned out the ritual and functional music of the local tribes who had lived in the settlement zones for thousands of years. In missionary efforts, translated hymns served as a "corrective" to what colonial settlers heard as the "unruly voices of Indigenous people."[45] In a scene from the U.S. historical TV series *1883,* the female protagonist plays Beethoven's "Moonlight" sonata on a piano that must be left behind on the plains, signaling a tearful farewell to European musical culture that did not generally take place.

At the same time, piano culture in the United States is much more diverse than European inheritance; blues, gospel, or jazz without the piano would be hard to imagine, as all these forms that originated in Black culture make innovative use of the instrument's percussive and tonal range. In the late nineteenth and early twentieth centuries, first ragtime and then boogie-woogie adapted European piano styles to blues-inflected music. Pianos brought to lumber and mining camps inspired the mostly improvised boogie-woogie music (in contrast to scored ragtime), also notable for its "percussive and blueslike" quality that favored "rhythmic contrasts rather than melodic or harmonic variations."[46] The piano slowly found its way into jazz ensembles, first imitating ragtime and boogie-woogie styles and then adapting trumpet signatures such as Louis Armstrong's "single-note line."[47] By the mid-twentieth century, the piano had become such an essential presence in jazz, gospel, and soul music that it is no surprise to find Aretha Franklin's baby grand—on which she recorded her 1967 breakthrough "I Never Loved a Man (The Way I Love You)"—enshrined in the former speakeasy in the legendary FAME Studios in Muscle Shoals, Alabama.[48] Though often (until recently) ignored in histories of art music in the United States, Black composers have long contributed symphonic, operatic, and piano repertoire, from the "Afro-Romanticism" of Florence Price's 1934 *Piano Concerto in One Movement* to the multigenre 2022 opera *Omar* by Rhiannon Giddens and Michael Abels.[49] All of this said, the piano's position in Black culture has often been an uneasy one, as exemplified in August Wilson's 1987 play *The Piano Lesson* (and its 2024 film adaptation), in which a family in the sharecropper era must decide what to do with their heirloom piano, which includes decorative carvings by an enslaved ancestor but could be sold to buy the land on which the family's forebearers labored. The piano itself aids in a violent exorcism, with its hammers striking copper wires with enough intensity to burn away not the piano but a troubling family ghost.

Outside the United States, pianos have taken on different post-European afterlives. In many official contexts, Western art music has been enshrined in hegemonic culture and used to demonstrate superiority. At the same time, music has sometimes signaled postcolonial identities that transgress clear binaries, transcending language but also in ways that have silenced Indigenous communities. For instance, Jane Campion's *The Piano* links music with muteness—not only in the protagonist's literal speechlessness but also in the sense that settler education (and with it, music) set out to silence Māori culture.[50] Here the instrument's journey into a Gothic vision of New Zealand carries both colonialist and anthropomorphic, erotic weight, undergoing a kind of reverse exoticization from a Native perspective when local Māori visitors start to pound on it.[51] Scenes like these show the "impossibility of upholding white, Western norms and values in places that are so different from the metropolitan home."[52] In the case of postcolonial Australia, unlike the United States, the abandonment of so many pianos in the wild indicates a failure of ideals of cultural superiority and a return to the instruments' sheer materiality, even as their colonialist durability continues. A "piano graveyard" in the bush near York, Australia, symbolically conveys this transition as detritus of colonial culture after the pianos' use in a Perth art installation left them without a place to go.[53]

Focusing on what remains and resounds in ruined pianos, not just romanticized images of them, is one way to keep their colonial origins troubling. Another and apparently opposite strategy makes a radical, defamiliarizing break between the piano's legacy and its remaining sounds. To do this requires seeing the piano as an intricate mechanism, removed from sonic conventions and treated as a more universal, versatile, adaptive, and migrating instrument. Annea Lockwood has noted this with reference to the postcolonial aspect of her work: "I came from an Anglo culture that walked into my country [New Zealand], in a very Victorian sense: domination over the environment. . . . The way I've worked with environmental sounds is exemplified by the sound itself as autonomous, a world unto itself."[54] This inheritance of a colonialist legacy gives Lockwood the luxury of playing with (and sometimes destroying) instruments while her sense of the wider environment has led her to swerve away from Eurocentric concert repertoire and toward the sounding of instrumental materials in their own right—returning from "qualified" to the more basic media types of structured sound.

Separating sounds from their hierarchical and ideological histories is of course a challenge. The term *affordance* helps in understanding how adhesive cultural associations can be. Introduced by James J. Gibson in 1979, the theory of affordances has shifted from debates among psychologists to applications in sociology, information systems, and the humanities.[55] In basic terms, "the notion of affordance provides a bridge between the social and the artefact,"[56] blurring the subject-object binary and making room for the web of associations that surround a song, for example, and depend on listeners' cultural backgrounds in interpreting what they hear. In media studies, *affordance* typically refers to the material qualities of a given medium, but when applied by musicologists, the term is used more in the cultural affordance sense, relating the physical properties of music to the contexts in which they sound. Music links people with common associations (from lovers' favorite songs to national anthems), amplifies ideological positions (as in a political rally), and even influences readiness to buy certain products (in advertising and shopping centers).[57] The physical properties of music—tempo, sonority, rhythm—affect human bodies in palpable and sometimes violent ways that are not necessarily connected to their cultural context. By tracing the material characteristics (the mechanics), sensorial experience (the dynamics and tempered tuning), and the spatiotemporal situatedness of instruments, we can describe connections between the piano as an object and its cultural affordances.

Several examples in literature provide a helpful lens for understanding the contingency of musical affordances, especially in postcolonial contexts. For the Trinidad-born narrator of Dionne Brand's memoir *A Map to the Door of No Return,* European music recalls painful childhood experiences of being marched into class in a stiff uniform to the sound of the "incessant, repetitive European classical music" that marked "the national culture" to which she could never—and never wanted to—belong.[58] Indigenous sound scholar Dylan Robinson has written on feeling "anxious" when hearing "cello, brass and percussion," whose "striving sound, taking space / leaves me less room to listen."[59] In Ojibwe novelist Louise Erdrich's *Last Report on the Miracles at Little No Horse,* a white woman's near-erotic relationship with her piano is violently ruptured by a flood. Swept away with her instrument's "revolving" in the "powerful vein," she wants to cling to its "cold, dead keys" but loses her grip, eventually finding her way to solid ground—and a new, gender-bent life on the reservation.[60] Unlike the flooded piano as a young white singer's lifeline in Taylor Swift's "Cardigan" video, this piano, an icon of colonialist culture, must be sacrificed.

Pierre Bourdieu's idea of habitus is also helpful in describing how cultural affordances work.[61] Composer Stefan Östersjö thinks of this concept as "a set of dispositions acquired through socialization processes" or "tacitly transmitted, embodied schemes and patterns," although "the specific social space, the objective conditions in which musical practice is socially constructed, is what Bourdieu would call a 'field.'"[62] From this perspective, a piano's habitus is the constellation of its sociocultural resonances, which manifest in each performance "field." The instrument's materiality mediates its associative meanings but is not dependent on them. From our intermedial perspective, the piano's material characteristics, sensorial experiences, and situatedness inform its meaning potential. When "transplanted" into a forest or pond, or when treated as an object to be burned, the piano is more than a cultural relic; it can be watched, heard, and even sounded (whether by humans or by other creatures) over a long period of time after its transplantation. Listening to improvisation on a decomposing piano also serves as a reminder that European concert music takes place in a finite time and place, in comparison to the hours-long, meditative performances of Indian classical music[63] or Indigenous musical rituals that run all night in the American Southwest. This defamiliarization of the piano makes it less bound to Eurocentric musical tradition and more open, as a medium, to new forms of listening.

In this chapter, we have described the piano's complex materiality and framed it in terms of radical and elemental media, beyond its role as a tool for making organized sounds. We have shown how, in the history of the piano's development, manipulating "natural" overtones and loading the instrument with cultural status have moved its materiality further from its botanical and mineral origins. The sheer size and weight of a grand piano holds a paradox of impressive materiality and expectations of sounds that transcend the earthly, similarly to the effects John Durham Peters has noted with regard to bells.[64] We have provided basic context for intermedial theory, which will inform our analyses in chapter 4, as distinct from media and communication studies that focus on media as socially determined content transmission. From Lars Elleström's perspective, the qualifying aspect of a sounding instrument leads to questions about how pianos are used and how, as a result of their materiality, these instruments have historically functioned differently from harpsichords, to showcase male genius and female domesticity (by keeping female bodies in the home practicing), all the while encoding Western "superiority" in colonialist contexts. Background on the piano's structure, tuning history, and socioeconomic affordances, as well as its extractivist and colonialist inheritances, has helped lay the groundwork for the following chapters on posthumanist and intermedialist approaches to decomposing pianos. Moving a piano from one habitat to another or radically defamiliarizing it through fire foregrounds the instrument's materiality and shows how it can work as a medium between physical sound waves and cultural norms.

3 DESTRUCTION, DECAY, AND ENTANGLED BODIES

In everyday life, we usually enjoy listening to the music we choose to hear. Music has a therapeutic potential in medical settings; in a choir or in a club, many experience music as something unifying. However, the situation changes when you cannot control the music that your neighbors or your teenagers enjoy, or when unwanted music plays on a speakerphone nearby. Your neighbor's music might be your noise pollution. But what about music and destruction? This connection emerges now and then as an unsettling, disruptive flip side of the ways we usually use music. A wide range of connections appears in myths (as in the satyr Marsyas's being flayed alive because he lost a music contest with the god Apollo), in music played to raise spirits on the battlefield or to drown out the noise of violence, and as a means of physical and psychological torture, as in Nazi concentration camps or in the United States–led prison in Abu Ghraib in Iraq. The hydraulis used to accompany Roman gladiator games with organ-like tones (a far more violent context than called up by the Hammond vibrato of American baseball), and even the disturbing sounds like "a furious monkey pounding on a broken piano" that were blasted from loudspeakers from North to South Korea[1] further destabilize ideas of music as a soothing or elevating force.[2] The long history of music enmeshed in violent conflict, experienced as acoustic violence, or used as sonic warfare are outside our project's scope but are important to note in a contextual framework.[3]

The use of operatic music in violent film scenes—for example, Stanley Kubrick's use of Rossini in *A Clockwork Orange* or the sonic force of

Wagner's "Ride of the Valkyries" in Francis Ford Coppola's *Apocalypse Now*—attests to music's sidelong history as a tool of domination. The intermedial mixing of rhapsodic or cheerful music with film violence has shifted from an innovative form of "counterpoint"[4] to a common trope used to build intensity on-screen, whether or not the music is strictly or partly diegetic, as in the speakers blaring from the helicopter in *Apocalypse Now.* If examined more closely, the contrast between music and violence in film (as well as in literature) not only critiques the sociopolitical co-opting of music but also exploits the ambiguity of clashing moral and aesthetic frameworks.[5] Likewise, in the performative act of decomposing instruments, music and noise become hard to tell apart, and conflicting frameworks of destruction and aesthetic experience start to oscillate.

Our focus in the first part of this chapter builds on our previous studies of music and violence to work more specifically with violence *on* musical materials. The act of burning or drowning a piano signals both aesthetic complexity and radical critique of human culture. If we think of *radical* in Richard Grusin's sense,[6] then this act places the instrument directly in relation to its physical environment—or even, in the sense of a piano made of wood, returns it to its source. We begin by discussing strong affective reactions to destroyed instruments in rock concerts and then in politically charged contexts, in contrast to works like Annea Lockwood's that take place in an avant-garde framework, based on the privilege of safety and the luxury of experimentation. We then draw on several theories of destroyed-instrument reception to explore questions of instruments as extensions of the human body. With this metaphor (which feels quite literal for many working musicians), we move into the question of bodily entanglement and decay in a posthumanist context.

Lockwood's "transplant" idea takes on posthumanist resonance not only by returning pianos to wood and ash through burning but also, in *Piano Garden* and *Piano Drowning,* which do not appear explicitly violent, by radically reorienting the piano into an outdoor space. In these cases, the decomposing instrument becomes entangled with processes of breakdown and transformation usually associated with plant or animal bodies. In a posthumanist perspective that decenters humankind and acknowledges its built-in tendency toward self-destruction,[7] along with new potentials for vulnerability and humility,[8] decay becomes an opening for reconsidering the role of musical instruments in human culture and for imagining more curious, ecologically embedded ways to approach a soundboard or keyboard.

On the Destruction of Instruments

The act of destroying musical instruments invites a wide range of responses. Outrage over the 2024 Apple iPad ad led to an apology from the company after a viral parody that reversed the trash-compactor action, reconstituting the piano and other artistic materials to the sound of a Bach fugue.[9] This reaction may have had as much to do with general anxieties about screen media and artificial intelligence incursions into creative work, as with the destruction of instruments themselves. In another arena, the frisson of audience pleasure mixed with distress in seeing a guitar smashed on a concert stage is well known. Pete Townshend's first, perhaps accidental cracking of his guitar's headstock led to his fame for smashing instruments on purpose, a kind of autodestructive ritual resulting partly from his study with artist Gustav Metzger.[10] Kurt Cobain's trashing of a Fender Stratocaster (and plenty of other valuable instruments, usually repaired) became part of his '90s grunge mystique.[11] Lady Gaga's unscathed emergence from a burning piano and smashed glass shards during the 2009 American Music Awards gave her added status as a sort of superhuman performer, as "the crowd whooped with delight."[12] The "Sixties rock mythology" incited by Jimi Hendrix's burning guitars and continuing through more recent performances with broken or burning instruments encompasses a sense of danger, showmanship, and "the romantic notion of rock'n'roll as a greater force than anything used to create it."[13] Even the image of Tori Amos's burning piano in *Boys for Pele,* a more indie iteration of instrument destruction, conveys a sense of empowerment, especially with the title's reference to the Hawaiian goddess of volcanic fire. These events and images seem less troubling than the unplanned destruction of instruments during airline travel, for example, or in the 2012 onslaught of Hurricane Sandy, which hit the Black Crowes' storage unit in New Jersey and destroyed all their instruments and equipment.[14]

Even in some artistic contexts, the fragility or creaturely quality of instruments can invite more sympathy than catharsis. In a 2019 studio visit, sculptor Jesse Darling describes dismantling a piano and linking it indirectly to the vulnerability of human bodies. "It seems sad, how easy it is to take a piano apart," he muses.[15] At the same time, a complex reaction including sympathy, awe, and distress is also possible. The piano-catapult scene in *Northern Exposure,* in which the instrument replaces the intended bovine sacrifice for art, brings up emotions ranging from relief (for the cow) to wonder at the piano's spinning arc in the air, and finally to shock as the piano crashes, clanging, to the ground. Sometimes a more party-like atmosphere takes over, as in a 2014 video of Annea Lockwood's *Piano Burning* in which audience members stand around the instrument, chatting as if around a bonfire; the piano's collapse leads to an excitement that some viewers—particularly musicians—might find painful.[16] The 2021 ISSUE Project Room film, in contrast, is more artfully edited and even ritualistic, with the audience out of view except for those at home in front of their pandemic-era screens, taking in the slow, even contemplative experience of a piano gradually burning to the ground.[17]

Destroying instruments in ideologically driven contexts incites far more shock and even trauma than live piano burnings do, though some might argue that there is no difference. Piano destruction sometimes leads to comparisons with iconoclasm or book burning. In the academic sphere, several musicologists have expressed concern about what kind of instrument is being damaged or simply find these artworks "heartbreaking."[18] Though some visual artists may see the act of destroying a piano as quite commonplace, whether as an act of material experimentation or as a symbolic critique of Eurocentric culture, others see it in a more ambiguous space. This ambiguity plays out in artworks that break down other cultural objects, including media. Visual and conceptual artist Paul Travis Phillips, for example, performs works that critique book bans in the United States by making cuts to physical books that, in the process, become complex, material works of art. Phillips also uses rust to tear away at his own paintings in a form of autodestructive art, but he points out that rust works both as a destructive and a protective agent, like a scab on damaged skin.[19]

While all these acts occur on a spectrum, there is a qualitative difference between the forced destruction of aesthetic materials and artistic acts of burning or breakdown. In cases such as Lockwood's *Piano Burning,* no authority figures have seized the instruments from musicians.

No enforcement of human behavior is at work, but rather an invitation to critical and affective response. In contrast, in 2023, photos emerged of the Taliban igniting a bonfire of musical instruments including guitars, a tabla (drum), and a harmonium, as well as speakers and amplifiers, in an effort to show the "immorality" of music.[20] After taking control of Afghanistan in 2021, armed Taliban members broke into the country's leading music school and destroyed classical string instruments, leading to the school's closure and students' fear of bringing their instruments home, in case the Taliban came searching "door to door." A 2014 suicide bombing outside one of the school's concerts had also targeted practicing musicians.[21] In Iran, music censorship by fundamentalist provincial leaders has led to canceled concerts and religious protests and raids, including violent attacks on singers, despite a reprimand from President Hassan Rouhani in 2015.[22] The situation has continued, with restrictions against most forms of music performance and production, prosecution of musicians in court,[23] and underground gatherings by composers and sound artists.[24]

Though these violent crackdowns on music-making come from different motivations than artistic experiments in privileged countries do, they are important to remember in order to contextualize art forms that ought not be taken for granted in a normative sense. Discomfiting ambiguities arise here as well. Audiences gathered around a burning piano may find the performance exciting; a religious extremist burning "instruments of sin" may enjoy the performative aspect of this destruction or experience a kind of catharsis.[25] Political acts of what might be called *sonoclasm* or *musicoclasm* can also be seen as the most extreme expression of a much broader suspicion of music's affective power. From Plato's warnings about the dangers of poetry and music to conservative Christian suspicions of singing, dancing, or even brass instruments in church, anxiety around music's power is not new. Links between rhythm and heartbeat, implicit in music's potential to entrain collective bodies in march beats or trancelike states,[26] is one reason *un*-metered harp music is effective in palliative care for the dying[27] and explains why some politically attuned composers have worked to disrupt lockstep rhythms as an act of resistance.[28] Instrument destruction in popular music concerts may be, on one level, an acknowledgment of music's power to escape human control and to affect the body in intensely palpable ways.

In the case of instrument destruction as performance, much less is personally at stake for the artists or musicians than it is under regimes that systematically destroy instruments or ban musical practice. At the same time, these performances may also work as a critique of hegemonic systems' use of music to dominate. For the audience, cultural affordances or *connotations* of artistic value, not a pregiven value, lead to a sense of shock, distress, or crime-scene curiosity for those used to experiencing pianos as representations of high culture. This response is not bound only to the aesthetic value of art music, however, because that value might be secondary in other contexts. As in Dionne Brand's *A Map to the Door of No Return,* colonialist uses of music would attach painful associations to a European instrument like a piano, which might seem worth a bonfire. Even this act could be both destructive and creative, however; as artist La Vaughn Belle has described her work with postcolonial cultural materials in the Danish West Indies, "We burn things sometimes to transform them."[29]

Piano burning is a particularly dramatic example of the wider phenomenon of destroying musical instruments, including but not limited to smashing guitars in rock concerts. Fluxus artists in the 1960s smashed violins (as in Nam June Paik's *One for Violin Solo*) and dropped pianos from tall buildings (as in Al Hansen's *Yoko Ono Piano Drop*), in addition to gentler performances such as Mieko Shiomi's Liszt played on a piano in a pond.[30] Frederic Rzewski's 1980 piano work *Winnsboro Cotton Mill Blues* adapts Pete Seeger's melody of the same title into an aggressive, palms-and-elbow-on-the-keyboard imitation of the textile machines that made for harsh working conditions in 1930s North and South Carolina; sometimes the pianist treats the instrument with such violence, it has to be retuned after the performance. In addition to showing the similarity of piano hammers to the mechanism of a cotton mill, not to mention risking damage to the instrument, this piece also calls attention to damaged human bodies. A particularly disturbing example of this metaphorical link is Christian Marclay's 1999 *Guitar Drop,* a video of a pickup truck dragging an amplified, "screeching" Fender Stratocaster for the same long thirteen minutes that white supremacists had dragged a Black man, James Byrd Jr., behind a truck in Jasper, Texas, the year before. As art critic Christina Rees puts it, whether the video is "successful" as art is beside the point; as a testament to racist violence, it is "excruciating, graphic, and exhausting."[31] Matteo Ravasio notes the ease with which one can link a guitar to a human body (it has a "neck" and a "body" of its own),[32] making this work an invitation to several levels of outrage.

Stephen Davies has argued that the shock value of these performative acts stems not only from the instruments' economic worth, practical use, or even cultural lineage but more importantly from what Ravasio reframes as "honorary person theory."[33] Musical instruments, Davies argues, are more than tools and invite an attitude of reverence that is not just due to their high monetary value.[34] As an extension of the musician's body, indeed nearly part of it, instruments take on physical, even erotic qualities; they are "held against the body, tucked into its crevices, or firmly grasped. They are placed in the mouth, or against the lips, or they are caressed by the hands." Thus the close personal relation between the musician and the instrument provides a piano, horn, or guitar with a status more like that that of a person who "deserves respect in their own right."[35] The piano offers particularly dramatic experiences of relational embodiment in its activation of affective presence through a combination of touch and hearing, communicated across acoustic space.[36] As experimental musician Bennett Hogg has found, even the proximity of an instrument to the playing body can link it in the same system of socially mediated vibrations; "the violin is a lie detector."[37]

In the ease of anthropomorphizing the piano, and in Dany van Dam's view of it as "erotic"/"exoticized" in postcolonial analysis of *The Piano* film,[38] the musical instrument's function as a body extension works in a dialogic and dynamic way. Though performance practices based on the nineteenth-century "genius" idea led to a standard of "disembodied" channeling of the composer by the pianist,[39] this phenomenon also (paradoxically) yielded deeply embodied, "hyper-sensation" responses, as in the case of Liszt and his female audiences.[40] Contemporary performers, especially when leaning into the piano in extended-technique pieces, often relish this double-bodied sense of music. In some cases, the performer may even experience a sense of a listening rather than performing role with the instrument as it surprises them with new sounds, as in Annea Lockwood's *Earwalking Woman.*

Body-instrument entanglement has been the subject of recent research on "4E cognition," which extends what we usually think of as neural thinking to include "embodied, embedded, enacted, and extended" forms of perception.[41] This approach acknowledges that cognition is enmeshed in bodies and environments; it is a concept that music educators can apply to better understand how human bodies become "embedded" or "extended" in their instruments.[42] The phenomenon of entrainment noted above, in which body rhythms synchronize with external beats,[43] further links music to embodied experience, making military marches and throbbing club music especially effective in sociopolitical bonding, for better or worse. Johnson and Cloonan speak of the double way in which music communicates, as both physical and aesthetic event, with the potential for violent resonances.[44] These phenomena help support Davies's claim that we react to instrument abuse much as we do to certain forms of human injury.[45] Davies compares this reaction with reactions to witnessing the injury of anesthetized bodies; although we know that the unconscious body can feel no pain, we still might flinch. Unlike body art that draws its intensity from both symbolic and actual inflicting of pain, instrument destruction does not evoke imagined pain but bears witness "to the injury" as the act of destruction itself.[46]

Pianos and Entangled Bodies

Bruno Latour's actor-network theory (ANT) is useful in conceptualizing the ties between sound waves and body, musician and instrument, listener and headphones. The idea of social systems working through "dissemination," rather than "purity" or "unity," imagines a "fibrous, thread-like, wiry, stringy, ropy, capillary character" creating multidimensional links.[47] With the help of ANT, Johann Larson Lindal demonstrates that a musical work is more than an abstract concept; its materiality becomes graspable in a network of actors, events, intermediaries, and mediators.[48] This concept aids in a metaphorical way as we describe various forms of sonic and material entanglements. From a posthumanist perspective, Claire Colebrook has applied Elizabeth Grosz's "volatile bodies" sense of corporeality as "something like an inhuman embodiment that gives itself through humans, but is also expressed in animal bodies, and the bodies of things."[49] Jane Bennett has explored similar ideas in her "vibrant matter" studies,[50] as has Stacy

Alaimo in her concept of "transcorporeality" that demands an ethics of "epistemological humility" between humans and nonhumans.[51] More recently, Daisy Hildyard has formulated "the second body," a complex of resonant links between individuals and power lines, medicines, pollutants, and other species.[52] As Latour notes, it is important to follow the "new associations" that are always forming in the "wild innovations" of collective actors.[53] These entangled actions are not "coherent" or "controlled"[54] but rather "borrowed, distributed, suggested, influenced, dominated, betrayed, translated."[55]

Though ANT does not clearly address habitual patterns of oppressive systems, it does aid in understanding constellations of bodies and materials in flux. The movements of musicians, instruments, sound waves, and listeners, changing their entanglements in surprising and even violent ways, are already more complex than they may appear, even in the conventional framework of the concert hall. This approach relates to Grusin's "radical mediation" and Peters's "elemental media" in the allowance for nonhuman "actants" (Latour's term, in the sense of "a source of action that can be either human or nonhuman") to interact in mediating/mediated relationships.[56] As "influence" or "translation" in ANT terms, the intermedial aspect of musical practice becomes clear as well; consider composers' adaptations of earlier works, the kinetic-performative lineage of Liszt, and the relationship of musical score to its embodiment onstage. In relation to our study here, the term *actants* can apply to human or nonhuman participants in the material modality (to return to Elleström's term as well) of musical destruction or decay. These actants can range from humans testing and documenting a decomposing piano in a pond to algae or frogs making a habitat inside it.

The embodied qualities of sounding musical objects are not restricted to musical instruments but also extend to secondary sound technologies, as Marshall McLuhan's nervous-system model of media would have it.[57] Rolf Goebel points out how musical recordings are often described as intimate experiences in literary texts and how sounding objects such as gramophones often gain transgressive, quasi-human, uncanny, or nostalgic agency. The engagement with musical sound when described on the page or when played back with technical devices, Goebel argues, calls for a counterpart. Recorded, "dead acoustic data" are reanimated when played back with technical devices such as gramophones and records.[58] Played on high-quality speakers, a historical recording of a choir in Vienna singing Bach just after World War II, for example, can sound almost frightening in its strange blend of heaviness and fragility.[59] At the same time, while the objects that play back music gain some quasi-human agency (or at least function as actants), there is a fundamental difference here, as the affective reaction to a burning tape recorder or a gramophone would not be the same as to a burning body or even a burning acoustic instrument.

In his article that builds on and critiques Stephen Davies's approach, Matteo Ravasio is not convinced by the explanation that we consider instruments as quasi individuals. He points out that an injured musician would be more subject to concern than his or her isolated arm or finger.[60] However, following Davies, notions of reverence toward the almost human bodies of musical instruments can convey something about the maltreatment of other nonhuman species such as rivers and trees—especially when the wood of a piano or guitar recalls its forest origins, or, on a larger scale, when nonhuman entities gain legal rights. The "elemental" transformation that occurs in a burning piano also recalls humans' "debt to fire," as John Durham Peters puts it; "fire is a jealous god and it calls for enormous expenditures and sacrifices."[61]

Ravasio proposes an alternative theory for the shock of a destroyed musical instrument: artistic value theory, which explains strong responses according to the instrument's special role in music-making as an art form. Unlike brushes and chisels or pens and typewriters, musical instruments are more than tools for producing artworks. They are part of the very artwork they help create. They are also objects of admiration for their level of craft and sound quality. This argument links pianos or violins to frescoes or sculptures in that "what has artistic value is to be paid a certain reverence and respect."[62] Perhaps this value even implies "love," as Ravasio notes in his only reference to Lockwood's *Piano Burning,* quoting (via Davies) a composer who responded, "Somebody must have loved that piano."[63] Here again we encounter the spectrum of instrument destruction, in which forced destruction happens at a remove from artistic experimentation but is not entirely divorced from it. On the one hand, headlines about the Taliban's destruction of the giant Bamiyan Buddhas created global outrage in 2001; on the other hand, more recent art attacks by climate activists have led to debates about cultural iconicity and what really matters when the world is burning.[64] When musical instruments are destroyed or damaged, this is different from the destruction of unique and specific artwork (the musical score remains), yet the affective resonances overlap.

Most importantly, Ravasio argues, pianos are more than objects to be looked at. Through their vital role in performing music in a concert hall, stage, or studio, they are involved in an intrinsically performative way in sounding human and instrumental bodies. In Ravasio's artistic value theory, a musical instrument acts as a material pars pro toto for musical experience. In this sense, the attraction and discomfort of watching a piano collapse is related to the aesthetic values and experiences that musical instruments actualize. Musical instruments represent the art not only produced but also performed with them specifically. While computers or pencils, brushes or paint are related to the production of literature or art, these objects do not necessarily evoke the experience of literature or art. Still, if only the aesthetic appreciation of art music prompts audiences to react to the destruction of musical instrument, this argument would also imply that everybody agrees on that aesthetic value. Even if people experiencing Lockwood's burning or drowning pianos may not feel a strong reaction to a culturally weighted object collapsing, they may respond to the piano's material structure at risk, as a quasi-living entity. One YouTube comment on the 2019 *Piano Burning* states, "I knew the snapping strings were coming but the anticipation was just too much to bear."[65] In different ways, both Ravasio and Davies describe musical instruments as more than functional tools. However, this perspective frames musical instruments not only as extensions of the performer's body or as intrinsic parts of the performance of the artwork but also as carriers of independent, almost human status. Anthropomorphizing pianos is nothing new. As Stuart Isacoff puts it in his history of keyboard temperament, "Today's piano is a miraculous machine: a colossus of cast iron and wood—filled with screws, hammers, and felt—weighing nearly a thousand pounds. Its frame sustains twenty-two tons of tension exerted on its strings—the equivalent of twenty medium-sized cars. Yet it can respond to the slightest whisper of a pianist's touch, producing a sound as warm and caressing as the human voice."[66] While attributing human qualities to instruments may seem to reinforce anthropocentric attitudes, it also opens a space to consider instruments in a wider context of aliveness. From an ecological standpoint, the piano's materiality, with all its extractivist history, links it to nonhuman life as well. The making of an instrument from wood implicitly reminds musicians and listeners alike that these carefully crafted bodies "continue to breathe, expand, and contract—vibrating as their environments change."[67] This vulnerability to natural conditions makes the piano's body as sensitive to homeostasis (or the lack thereof) as a human, fox, or tree. Lockwood's own point about the piano as an "instrument designed for maximum control" relates on one level to associations between classical music and discipline,[68] but it also denotes the paradox of fragility and extreme tension in a piano's design. To loosen or break apart the hammer mechanisms and pressurized wires inside a piano's body is similar to an assault on any living vascular or nervous system—and thus moves beyond human cultural conventions.

Posthumanism and Decaying Pianos

The act of burning or drowning a piano occurs in the ambiguous zone between human and nonhuman, creating another layer of complexity beyond music and violence. It also activates ambiguity between intentional destruction and more passive decay, as both occur at different points and speeds depending on whether a human sets the instrument on fire or places it outdoors. Either way, the decomposition of a piano into wood that can burn or decay strips it of its usual affordances and places it on an equal footing with the rest of the forest, pond, or field. Any experience of cultural loss becomes a natural loss as well, and vice versa; as Mikkel Krause Frantzen notes, "A loss of nature is by definition also a loss of culture, culture understood as a life-form."[69] To understand instruments as a form of more-than-human entanglement, we apply the lens of posthumanism to music, inviting a less anthropocentric take on burning and drowning pianos. We then move from destruction to decay as we view decomposing instruments in a process of cultural-to-ecological transformation.

In a broad sense, *posthumanism* refers to a decentering of human exceptionalism in favor of the view that "the posthuman subject . . . is embedded in its natural environment, inextricably linked to the animals and vegetation around, and fused with technology."[70] Art theorist T. J. Demos has noted that such a reorientation opens human subjects to "multinatural" experiences.[71] One of the central challenges of posthumanism is to conceptualize a relation between the human being and its environment that is not based on received binaries such as subject/object, human/animal, or culture/nature. Of course, *posthumanism* is itself a human construct, like the influential if contested term *Anthropocene*. Even *posthuman* as a word cannot quite move beyond the human self-centeredness it strives to overcome. So how can one conceptualize the nonhuman in a way that it is not perceived directly in difference, as other to human? As environmental humanities scholar Scott Slovic points out, the effort to overcome anthropocentrism is daunting and perhaps even impossible ("we can't really think like a stone, but it helps us to imagine what it would be like to think like a stone").[72] To pretend, as John Durham Peters has posited, that humans are on equal footing with any other species on this planet would be to downplay or ignore the massive destructive impact of human activities on other species.[73] Works like Annea Lockwood's *Piano Transplants* expose the difficulty of posthumanizing cultural materials while at the same time showing a renatured piano's surprising power to provoke more entangled thinking.

Many efforts to relate posthumanism to human-made sound fall into familiar ecocritical habits of textual or musical analysis without more radical reflection. Stefan Sorgner's contribution to *The Bloomsbury Handbook of Posthumanism*, for example, frames Wagner's Gesamtkunstwerk as a structural posthumanism analog "because it embraces and uses all facets of life, even the traditional audience gets included, which is very much in the spirit of pre-theater dramatic works."[74] Moving into "cyborg music" and touching only briefly on Björk's "creation of new instruments,"[75] the essay's overall argument does not engage fully with musical materiality and fails to escape either the literary-critical model or the anthropocentric idea of technological progress. Some concerts and experiments linking digital technology to acoustic instruments do challenge received ideas of the nature/culture binary, but even recent studies on "rethinking the musical instrument" or "eco-örganology" tend to focus more on synthesizers and wearable technologies than on deeper reconsiderations of instruments' materiality in the biological world.[76] Studies and experiments that take that entanglement into account, by musicians and artistic researchers Stefan Östersjö, Sabine Vogel, and Julia Adzuki, will figure into our discussion later in this book.

A posthumanist perspective on burning and drowning pianos is useful mainly in loosening anthropocentric, binary-driven approaches to music. While, in Davies's approach, musical instruments appear as stand-ins for human bodies, and in Ravasio's approach as materializations of art, the relation between musician and instrument also invites us to consider these instruments in more-than-human context. The new materialist aspect of posthumanism contains "an ontological reorientation that . . . conceives of matter itself as a lively or as exhibiting agency" related to Peters's mediating forces.[77] In Emanuele Coccia's more rhapsodic terms, "Life is always the reincarnation of that which is not alive, a cobbling together of mineral elements, a carnival of the telluric substance of a planet."[78] If pianos work as performative matter, they can take on a creaturely quality beyond the concert hall or living room. If the piano not only connects the human body with musical sounds but also with musical machinery, this enmeshment relates to Donna Haraway's concept of the cyborg as technology and body being closely linked.[79] The instrument's collapse is transformative not in the sense of a broken robotic extension of the human, however, or in the flattening sense of the Apple trash-compactor ad, but rather in its yielding to the ecological "carnival" from which it came.[80] The implicit critique of human cultural hegemony in Lockwood's works, as well as in Ross Bolleter's ruined-piano explorations in Australia, is an invitation to imagine human-made instruments as part of a larger shared ecological context.

Several other strains of posthumanist thought are helpful in addressing the decomposition of instruments. One approach, beyond the linear trajectory of Rosi Braidotti's "critical posthumanism," which draws on postcolonialist and feminist models to critique the "monadic Enlightenment subject," is to think backward, dedomesticating and defamiliarizing human cultural phenomena.[81] In his posthumanist approach to music, Gary Tomlinson argues that if one avoids the temptation to anthropomorphize birdsong, for example, it is possible instead to hear the reverse: human song-making as related to nonsyntactic animal processes, such as "dedicated neural networks, intergenerational pedagogy, practice, and sheer energy expenditure," even if some "trans-species capacities remain to us obscure."[82] As we have already noted, a relatively new approach is to relate posthumanism to intermediality, which is based on the argument that nonhuman species also engage in complex interactions with their environments and with each other, with meaning-making potential in biology and materiality, a "semiotic continuum between nature and culture."[83]

If Jane Bennett's "'vital materiality' runs through and across bodies, both human and nonhuman,"[84] then it also breaks down the life/matter distinction.[85] This blurring of human, animal, and thing thus hints at the entropic vulnerabilities of a body or a piece of wood. Underlying this move is a willingness to accept the failure of the human cultural project itself, whether in terms of its inability to cure or care for the larger world or in terms of its future demise. Claire Colebrook's approach to posthumanism, in which humankind already holds the capacity for its own failure *at* being human (along the lines of Adorno and Horkheimer's *Dialectic of Enlightenment*), goes so far as to consider Homo sapiens to be a "parasitic" species, something beyond the simply predatory: "it lives only in its robbing and destruction of a life that is not its own."[86] Following Adorno and Horkheimer, who held that Nazi barbarity arose from, not in spite of, the very culture that had enshrined Goethe and Beethoven,[87] Colebrook's perspective asks for a radical reconsideration of the arts and humanities: "Today, in a century that can begin to sense, if not articulate, humanity's capacity to destroy its own species-being, along with the milieu that it has constitutively polluted to the point of annihilation, what sort of defense might one make for the future of humanities disciplines?"[88] If humankind is a parasite, she writes, its "inflections do not just radiate outward and create local distortions but *deterritorialize* or become inflections of the whole, capable of infecting or polluting every other line of system or parasitism."[89]

The term *deterritorialization* is invasive in Colebrook's sense. According to this model, a burned or drowned piano would signal inevitable collapse of high culture devouring itself, or at least serve as a reflection that novelist Jennifer Croft has put this way: "Every artwork, even something as sublime as a symphony, arose at the expense of a forest, or a tundra, or a desert, or a stream."[90] This view (even if posited by a semireliable narrator) is certainly part of the picture. But it negates the entanglement of human-crafted materials and the ecosystems from which they come, as well as the potential for human change in "loosening" (to use Annea Lockwood's word) anthropocentric control. As Christine Daigle has argued, "the human we need to see extinct is the humanist concept of the human, not the human itself."[91] There can be pleasure, not just punishment, in imagining human cultural spaces invaded by other, outdoor ecosystems, as theatre scholar Vicky Angelaki has done in Vienna's Kunsthistorisches Museum: "What if debris suddenly exploded everywhere, the Roman statues now resting on a surface of scattered leaves and fallen branches? . . . What if wildlife creatures roamed the corridors with the same ease as the affluent tourists?"[92] In an imaginative leap in the opposite direction, what if pianos took on the ruminative attitude of cows in a pasture, as in Samuel Barber's lilting song set to the Jerzy Harsymowicz poem "A Green Lowland of Pianos"?[93]

The term *deterritorialization* contains another inflection that allows for more than simply grim acceptance of—or even Malthusian pleasure in—humankind's often cruel and ultimately self-destructive culture. The term takes on a more descriptive than prescriptive role in Elizabeth Grosz's thinking about sound in the nonhuman world. Drawing on Darwin's mapping of various species' mating patterns through sound, biosemiotician Jakob von Uexküll's idea of the *Umwelt,* or "life-world," and Deleuzian models of music's affective power in nature, Grosz has theorized a vibratory complex in which "the very bodies of organisms are the instruments" and "art is of the animal" as "the unexpected, unpredictable effect, of the coupling of a milieu or territory with a body."[94] This perspective includes humans in the messy, noisy tangle of the world, for all our parasitic tendencies. For all the "anxiety" associated with posthumanism, rethinking the human in terms of more complex mappings allows us to "acknowledge the materiality of our entanglements" to see how "materiality and subjectivity are radically intertwined," as Daigle puts it.[95] Her approach to posthumanism in terms of "vulnerability" finds those points where decay can disorient humans from our need for control, certainty, and permanence in a productive way: "We do not experience ourselves as the fleeting beings we are" when in fact we are "tenuous embodied selves."[96]

Artists who cultivate decay, in works such as Beverly Buchanan's 1981 *Marsh Ruins,* an elusive system of eroding concrete and tabby on the Georgia coast in the United States, often find that "entropy can best be described as possibility" as the process of decay adds more biological factors to a given system.[97] In terms of a musical instrument, decomposition can also add new and unexpected sounds. As coauthor Heidi Hart has observed in her work with a found harpsichord, stored in a basement for thirty-five years, the instrument may look intact on the outside, but internally, moth-eaten felt, loosened strings, and a cracked soundboard make stranger sounds than what one would expect in a Baroque-style keyboard instrument. For all their long-untuned fragility, the string "choirs" yield surprisingly robust glissandi when strummed (or struck with dulcimer hammers), with overtone whistles along the damaged soundboard. Dried moth wings shiver under the vibrating strings. Some of the keys still release tonal sounds, depending on the day's temperature and humidity, while others simply thrum like a percussion instrument. This decaying instrument made in 1980s Leipzig, associated with long-ago aristocratic chamber concerts as well as with cultural traditions maintained in the former East Germany, is now a vulnerable mesh of wood, strings, metal, and bits of plastic and felt as the delicate system of plucking mechanisms breaks down. It makes less organized and more creaturely, weather-dependent sounds than it was designed to, yielding new possibilities for improvisation. Frequent soundings by the household cats, testing the keys or tapping the strings, give it a surprising more-than-human function as well. This is hardly a dead instrument, still capable of clicking, thrumming, and the occasional resonant tone.

Even a burning piano still vibrates (if most notably in the dramatic snap of a copper wire) in Annea Lockwood's performances that both burn the piano and record its sounds; a piano settled into a pond or forest will still respond to weather and touch, whether human or not. The vibratory bond with a musician's body becomes enmeshed in other forces too. To quote Deleuze and Guattari, who in turn cite the birdcall-obsessed composer Olivier Messiaen, "music is not the privilege of human beings: the universe, the cosmos, is made of refrains; the question in music is that of deterritorialization permeating nature, animals, the elements, and deserts, as much as human beings."[98] The forces of entropy and even violence, which Grosz's model does not fully take into account, are also a part of this shifting dynamic of territory and vibration. The ambiguity between decay and transformation is what makes works like Annea Lockwood's powerful, as they show the inherent cost of breaking out of one familiar habitus and into a new one. They also expose both the cost and possibility of literal breakdown, whether at the speed of fire or at the slower tempo of rising water and spreading vines. This move from the musician–piano connection to a more complex and unpredictable mesh of elements and other life-forms gives the instrument a posthumanist representational power beyond its familiar cultural affordances. It may show the self-destructive tendencies of human-made culture, but it also reveals new possibilities for more-than-human listening and sound-making.

Burning or drowning a piano, or watching a long, slow film of its demise, does more than simply reenact a Fluxus-style performance from the mid-twentieth century. This is also a more complex process than Ólafur Elíasson 2018 *Ice Watch* enacting ice slowly melting in an urban setting, with its obvious signaling of threatened glaciers. The sonic component of listening to a piano's collapse, in addition to the visual processing of time, makes the experience palpable in its unpredictability. In this sense, Lockwood's works are more in line with Richard Skelton's buried and "exhumed" violin, to which he attached microphones to hear the "unplayable husk," allowing for decay or destruction, and listening with more curiosity than the need to control.[99] They also relate to Ruth Ewan's 2012 project performing a ritual sacrifice of drowning instruments (including a burning piano) in a lake that will become a future peat bog, "echoing prehistoric burial techniques."[100] Lockwood's *Piano Transplants* evoke ritual connections between culturally invested objects and the environment; they recall the close historical relationship between music and violence; they critique the piano as a representation of tradition, high culture, and human performativity; they deterritorialize instruments into more-than-human ecosystems; finally, these works transform the instruments through the process of decay.

Piano decomposition performs the posthumanist shift of decentering the human, however challenging that is to do. If classical music in particular has come into question for its colonialist and white supremacist underpinnings, and if human music-making in general—even less privilege-tainted forms like pop and jazz improvisation—can be accused of anthropocentrism, burning a piano may also convey a cleansing impulse for those asking what good the arts can do when Mother Earth herself is burning. In light of "toxic" aspects of the European musical legacy,[101] Lockwood's transplant idea works as a form of radical re-contextualization and "alienated understanding of what it means to be human."[102] At the same time, ideas of human parasitism like Claire Colebrook's may be too limiting in imagining what is possible for post-humanist instruments. Experiments with burning and decaying pianos allow humans to see and hear the rest of the world more clearly, with human sound-making as a part of that complexity.

4 MEDIA AND MATERIAL TRANSFORMATIONS

To this point, our project has shown how a musical instrument can function as a medium in its own right through its material and cultural resonances. We have described instrument decomposition in different contexts and from historical and posthumanist perspectives. In this chapter, we trace the perceptual shifts that can occur through artistic performances of piano destruction and decay; they expose material aspects of the instruments usually taken for granted. This defamiliarizing of human cultural materials is an important aspect of posthumanist musicology[1] and allows for new intermedial understanding as well.

As we have discussed, both Stephen Davies and Matteo Ravasio propose reasons for strong affective responses to a destroyed instrument, through its identification either with the performing musician or with artistic value.[2] Both touch on the quasi-bodily aspects of instruments. Davies's approach echoes media theorist Marshall McLuhan's definition of media as extensions of the human,[3] calling attention to close interplay between performer and instrument. Ravasio highlights the instrument's role as an intrinsic part of music, just as a dancer's body is part of the dance. But neither Davies nor Ravasio focuses on the consequences of this quasi-bodily perspective, which our intermedial approach sets out to do.

Focusing on the role of media in communication challenges us to focus on objects and processes that are easy to overlook when perceiving content in everyday use. Media and their affordances seem transparent as long as they are familiar and functional, and as long as they do not call attention to themselves but provide immersive access to the content or the message. Sybille Krämer compares media to a messenger standing right in front of us, calling attention to an absent person's words but not the messenger's individuality.[4] We can also apply this thinking to conventional musical performance. At a piano recital, the instrument is center stage, but the audience might focus primarily on the sounds they hear, attributing them to a composer, musical genre, or period. In today's hypermarketed concert culture, in which performers are expected to express themselves through their clothing and gestures, even the piano's sounds may become secondary. The instrument, as a medium messenger in Krämer's sense, is such an intrinsic part of live musical performance that its material shaping of musical experience is not always obvious. When musical instruments are foregrounded as objects, valued for their intricate mechanics and special sonorities (in the case of a Stradivarius, a Steinway, or a period instrument, for example), they gain back some of their material, mediating power. But in most situations, the instruments remain transparent technical media, mere tools that provide the sounds we expect them to make.

At the same time, instruments are actants in a complex musical network of human and nonhuman bodies. Relations among composer, performer, instrument, sound, and score have changed across genres and time periods. When we think of instrumental jazz musicians, we may expect a collaborative and improvisational practice; singer-songwriters may evoke a more subjective, individualistic presence. However, one characteristic of all music—whether heard at an outdoor festival or in a conventional concert hall—is entrainment, the way human body rhythms can align with musical beats.[5] This material-sensorial entanglement may not be as direct in filmed or recorded performance but can certainly occur through loudspeakers in a club, where dancers feel the bass pulse in their bodies, or in a military setting, when musical rhythm keeps marching bodies in line. Many concertgoers may take this entanglement for granted, especially if they expect to appreciate the music on a cognitive or emotional level, but they may not understand their own physical reactions to it. A 2023 article for classical music audiences, on the attunement of heart and breath rates to musical meter, surprised some readers who had not considered this possibility.[6]

In the context of popular music, physical connections between bodies and environments play out in obvious ways. Singing along with the performer, jumping in rhythm with the music, and loosening inhibitions with various substances link the audience's bodies to those of the artists onstage. Within the conventions of classical music, however, the audience is expected to sit still, not to applaud between movements of a symphony or concerto, and (despite some performers' openness to change) to keep cell phones tucked away. In the nineteenth-century paradigm of absolute music, the performer's bodily presence was traditionally downplayed (the extremely gestural performance style of composer-pianist Franz Liszt aside), though concert conventions were looser than they are today. Not only the instrument but also the performer was seen as a tool, a vessel, a "technical medium of display"[7] whose task it was to provide access to the musical (often male) genius of the composer. As a result, and even in some cases in today's culture of Instagrammable performers, the physical effort of producing classical music often remains transparent and has to be highlighted with force—for instance, by pushing performers to their physical limits, emphasizing fashion choices, or exaggerating emotional gestures.[8] Contemporary music performances that feature a prepared or "inside" piano offer another way to foreground the performer, but in that case more as a facilitator, with the instrument as a dramatic material presence onstage.

The decomposition of musical instruments appears to work in a similar direction. It moves our attention away from the cultural values attached to the piano and away from conventional sonic expectations, toward a material intricacy that we otherwise take for granted. When Stephen Davies describes instruments undergoing destruction, he foregrounds "the musical instrument [as] the locus of damage" rather than the agent's role in causing it.[9] We extend this approach to show how artistically disruptive use of media self-reflexively calls attention to their presence—and to media in a more "radical" or even "elemental" sense, as Richard Grusin and John Durham Peters have theorized in different ways.[10] Instruments under duress not only represent human culture but also emphasize the materiality of sounds and structures by putting them at risk and revealing their vulnerability.

When we follow the radical treatment of instruments all the way to its ecological end, however, this destructive aspect loses part of its threatening potential. If piano wood can transform into fuel or insect fodder, its destruction is also regenerative. The instrument's cultural affordances (if culture is understood as a "life-form" in Mikkel Krause Frantzen's sense[11]) can also grow new shapes and meanings when the object itself, as medium, collapses. Thus, we argue that these acts of destruction not only convey something about the artistic or ethical values that Davies and Ravasio address but also expose music as a human construct in a more-than-human world. When moved out of the conventional spaces, renatured and decomposing instruments enact other connections than among performer, instrument, and audience in favor of new spaces, nonhuman beings, and surprising sounds. We explore these new entanglements with specific attention to the layers of mediation in Annea Lockwood's *Piano Transplants.*

Piano Transplants

Annea Lockwood's *Piano Transplants* provide not only a shift of perception but also a radical physical move: a transplantation of instruments out of their protected cultural sphere and its conventions. (Even Lady Gaga's burning-piano spectacle noted earlier took place in an indoor performance space.) In her work, Lockwood strives to create radical and nonhierarchical sound experiences with a "focus on elemental and natural sound sources."[12] These experiences displace the traditional focus on human performance in favor of a posthumanist perspective that allows for interactions between the instrument and weather, water, plant life, and fire.

The following analysis traces the roles of elemental change, material process, and media transformation in the 2021 ISSUE Project Room films of *Piano Burning, Piano Garden,* and *Piano Drowning.* Though audiences can experience live mediation of music in a performance setting, it is a rarer occurrence to witness artworks that involve the destruction or decay of instruments without the double mediation of audiovisual technology. The following analysis shows that this additional transmediation of Lockwood's performances does not necessarily prevent embodied experience of these works and the ecological entanglement they perform. Lars Elleström's media modalities reveal how these films' material, spatiotemporal, sensorial, and semiotic aspects involve the spectator's body, allowing for affective responses and new forms of meaning-making.

Our analysis also includes levels of radical and elemental mediation that move beyond the contexts of conventionally qualified media types such as (art) music. Drawing on Peters, we discuss the roles of fire, air, and water as elemental media interacting with the piano, with additional reference to Richard Grusin's radical mediation. We show in detail how the 2021 films transmediate these elemental aspects of live performance and, on the audiovisual level, a performative experience within the media-specific affordances of film. The ISSUE Project Room's two-and-a-half-hour-long film of the three performances is an experience of slow watching and careful listening. Our fine-grained intermedial analysis takes the time needed to focus on the objects and beings we interact with, the sense data we focus on, and how all of these aspects contribute to unexpected forms of perception through decomposing pianos.

Piano Burning

This one-hour, eleven-minute video transmediates a performance of Annea Lockwood's *Piano Burning* at the 2021 Brisbane Festival, featuring a performance by composer and artist Vanessa Tomlinson. When we approach *the material modality* of the film, the act of looking for objects and beings that offer communicative interfaces makes processes of mediation more obvious. The scene includes an upright piano placed in a circle of earth or sand in front of a wall, a performer, a person who acts as a fire starter, and fire itself. The fire's rapid spread and crackling sounds suggest the presence of fire accelerant and microphones. The fire's transformational qualities expose the piano's materials: wood eventually transformed into charred embers (from 0:15:05), the piano's internal wires, and the cast-iron harp revealed as the wood falls away (from 0:15:20).

In the *sensorial modality,* we notice *visual, auditory,* and *audiovisual* events. As the piano fades into the frame, it appears center stage but at the same time out of place in what looks like an industrial area. The performer slowly walks into the frame and sits in front of the keyboard as a man sets the piano alight from its back and leaves. The fire spreads quickly, the starting signal for a short improvised performance;

the keyboardist adjusts her movements not primarily to produce music but to avoid flames and smoke. She moves toward the lowest end of the keyboard as the upper range becomes too hot, and there she continues to play. When the heat forces her to leave the seat, she must let go and leave the scene where the burning piano remains center stage (0:05:28).

In the following interplay of piano and fire, we notice different visual transformations. The upright piano emitting flames (instead of musical sounds) (Figure 1) turns into a simple rectangular container for fire, slowly opening to reveal the cast-iron frame with copper wires protruding like harp strings, an instrument within the instrument, or the ribs of a skeleton (notably around 0:18:00). The piano turns into a simple wooden and increasingly charred box that eventually collapses (0:38:10) (Figure 2). As the flames decrease, from violent yellow-orange to red-orange against the increasingly dark background of nightfall, we notice sparks and trailing smoke (from 50:00) and the piano's amber glow in contrast to the neon lights of what looks like a gas station further off (1:00:06). Finally, all that remains of the piano is a smoldering pile of wood and metal with undistinguishable form. The film ends with an extreme close-up of the glowing embers and fades out.

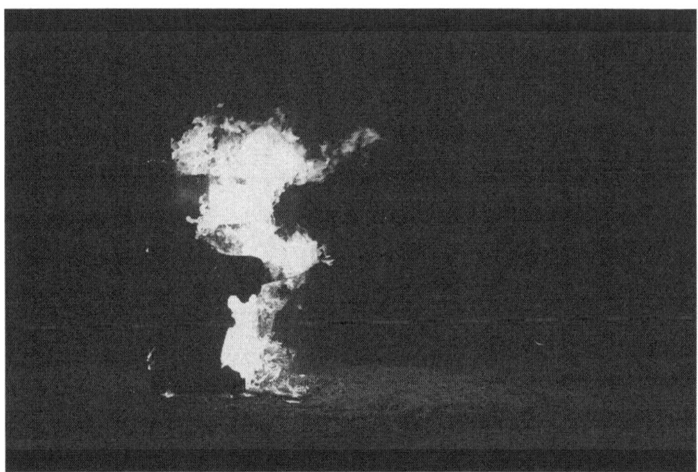

Figure 1. The piano emitting flames but also shaping the fire. Annea Lockwood's *Piano Burning,* 2021, presented as part of Brisbane Festival 2021, Lawrence English (Room40). Image courtesy of ISSUE Project Room.

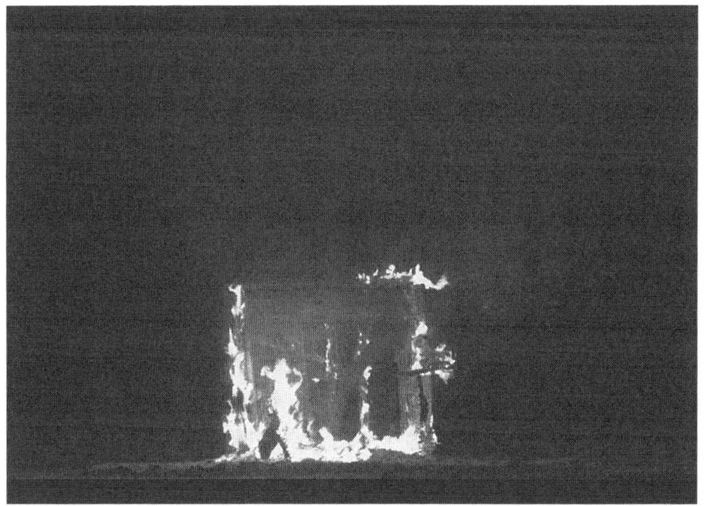

Figure 2. The "harp" visible inside the charred wooden frame that soon collapses. (ca 38:00). Annea Lockwood's *Piano Burning,* 2021, presented as part of Brisbane Festival 2021, Lawrence English (Room40). Image courtesy of ISSUE Project Room.

Different sorts of *sounds* enter one by one as well. The rush of car traffic draws attention to the auditory mode even before the piano fades in. These traffic sounds are then drowned out by the roar of an airplane (0:02:05), which eventually merges with the clearly audible (electronically amplified) crackling of burning wood and the noticeably out-of-tune piano during the improvised performance. The pianist begins with broken, dissonant chords across the keyboard's range and ends with a percussive bass pattern that includes fewer and fewer notes. The sounds of burning wood and music from the same object create a sense of ambiguity, especially as the burning piano destabilizes the keys' volume from one to the next. The sense of fine-tuned control expected in live piano performance falls apart. When the music stops, the fire continues to produce sounds, from the aggressive roaring of a bonfire to a calmer crackling that allows other sounds to protrude again: easily identifiable noises such as car and occasional airplane traffic, the murmur of an invisible audience, and later birds, sounds which could possibly be crickets, and shuddering noises along with what may be the aeolian harp-like hum of the remaining copper wires (ca. 1:00:24).

Other sensory modes of the live event, notably the heat and the smell of burning wood (with accelerant and varnish) cannot be directly conveyed by audiovisual media. We do get a sense of the heat from the performer's movements. On site, we might be more conscious of the performer's body and its vulnerability to the fire. In this media transformation, the distinct and electronically amplified sound of burning wood transmediates the fire's dramatic and potentially threatening force, as well as its diminishing heat. The more the fire burns down, the nearer close-up shots come to the burning wood and glowing embers, creating intimacy with the heat that becomes less dangerous as it smolders to ash. In the sensorial modality, the burning piano may start with spectacular sights but guides its audience into close listening that extends the familiar experience of a domesticated fire, as fire and piano sound together in unpredictable ways. The short improvised performance and the piano's shape draw attention to the auditory modes that involve us in listening to rather than watching a fire.

In the *spatiotemporal modality,* we notice transformative negotiation between the space and time of the performance and their transmediation into one hour of film. The performance site remains obscure and anonymous but conveys the audiovisual impression of an industrial area close to a major traffic artery and an airport. Some movements occur on site, from the improvised performance to the piano's fiery collapse. The film's editing adds an extra dynamic level by switching among mostly fixed or slowly moving close-ups, full shots, and increasingly wide shots slowly fading into each other. When the on-site process slows down, the editing increases in tempo as it switches angles more frequently. The time it takes to burn a piano into a heap of glowing embers and ash is summed up both through elliptical cuts and indexical signs of cyclical time, from dusk to darkness and a final close-up of glowing embers. Through the continuous changes caused by the fire and the changing of perspectives (most notable at 0:22:30), there is a sense of losing time while watching and listening; one hour does not feel long at all, yet time also seems to slow and stretch, as if in the passage of a long night. The live piano burning described in our final chapter does not take as long as this filmed version appears to, though the actual time of viewing is only one hour.

In the *semiotic modality,* the film destabilizes art-music expectations, materially by the outdoor, industrial environment, and audiovisually by the sights and sounds of the fire competing with the pianist. The performance is short and leaves little space for a more informed understanding of what is musically expressed here, though the movement from broken chord clusters to the pounding of the bass keys (reminiscent of Fredric Rzewski's *Winnsboro Cotton Mill Blues*) does enact a shift from modernist sounds to more machinelike gestures. Even for viewers used to performance art, the whole process sets up and then unhinges musical meaning potential. For instance, the fact that the performer moves to the lowest section of the bass is ambiguous; it is indexical both in that it evokes an existing piece of music *and* in that it responds contingently, as movement forced by the flames' heat and smoke. The space and time of the performance also appear contingent in relation to the processes of fire. Any iconic or symbolic meaning potential is partly intentional and partly accidental, more found than produced. Sounds lose their cultural affordances, expressing instead something of radical mediation in Grusin's terms, or a relational process in the very fact of material, fuel, and body responding to each other.

The conventions of musical performance may also affect how some viewers hear the fire, not only as noise but as aesthetically framed sounds, and as a continuation of the performer's improvisation. We find some iconic relationships in the visual transformation of the piano, from an instrument emitting flames (instead of sounds), to a bonfire in the shape of a piano, then to a container, a frame, and finally to a ruin. The most iconic relation arises from the strings' metal frame and its resemblance to a harp or ribs. Depending on which meaning we choose, this body-like shape might signal either a surprise revelation or a violent death, or perhaps both at the same time. For some viewers, however, after the piano's collapse into firewood and embers, symbolic and iconic resemblances may recede into the background. The focus remains on the fire and on its transformation as a symptom of passing time. Semiotically, the performance highlights the piano's materiality, auditory experience beyond musical conventions, shifting iconic associations, and the blurry entanglement of music, sounds, and noise.

When we move to the level of elemental and radical media, *Piano Burning* not only changes and expands notions of music but also draws attention to fire as a medium. As we have discussed with regard to musical instruments, fire in this performance is not used to produce lights, warmth, tools, or social connections; nor is it out of control as an elemental force. Instead, the performance foregrounds ambiguous relationships of fire to organic life and human civilization. John Durham Peters presents the element of fire as the first human tool, a "medium as well as the precondition for almost all human-made media."[13] Even if fire itself is not a survivable environment for living beings, it enables human civilization. Humans depend on fire to carve out their habitat, to produce light and warmth—to the extent that Peters remarks that "human beings are pyrophytic plants: we grow together with fire."[14] Combustion is the hidden motor of our organic life, as "every cell in our body is slowly burning."[15] Domesticated fire is built into many layers of human civilization, from a home hearth to our use of oil to the electricity-driven internet. Terms like *global heating* and *burning planet* indicate the close relationship of fossil fuel–based fire to climate emergency. However, fire in itself is "fragile" in that it depends on the right combination of oxygen, fuel, and other conditions.[16] Thus, the medial perspective toward fire is a contradictory one. Human civilization contains fire and is threatened by it as soon as it gets out of control.[17]

Piano Burning showcases fire as an ambiguous mediator of human life. In the performance, the destructive potential is not entirely neutralized or tamed (as it is in candles, torches, or electricity sockets). Instead, the performance enacts symbiotic interdependences. In the *material modality,* the fire pushes all cultural and musical affordances of the piano into the background, highlighting the piano's role as firewood and fuel. In its use as fuel, Peters calls fire "a contradiction itself. It destroys what it touches but also destroys itself."[18] Humans turn fire into a tool by containing it, by offering fuel in a controlled environment. Thus, the burning piano displays fire as human medium but in a defamiliarized way. In the *sensorial modality,* the performance presents a controlled fire on one level as flames in shifting colors that we would recognize from a campfire, bonfire, or wildfire. At the same time, the very construction of the piano, along with electronic amplification, frame the fire aesthetically into surprising shapes and cinematic sounds as the wood and metal crack and whine and collapse.

On site, the fire would engage smell and touch as well. Apart from humans' use of lights, smoke, and electrical technologies to communicate, Peters points toward a "baseline of evocative vagueness" that is characteristic of fire, that conveys "no special message besides its burning, pulsing self."[19] This experience is familiar from the meditative experience of a burning campfire, but here it is once again defamiliarized (without the smell of smoke) and foregrounds only visual and audiovisual experience. Following the performance emphasizes the *space* that fire occupies and its ephemeral relation to *time,* as it "exists by disappearing."[20] In this respect, fire is similar to musical sounds. The staged process of transformations, of a piano into firewood, the wood into charcoal, and the charcoal into ashes, takes a specific amount of time. The film transmediates a distinct experience of the on-site performance, although it speeds up the process. In fact, we may be better able to focus on this transformation in its edited form.

Overall, *Piano Burning* demonstrates the role of fire as a multisensory catalyst. It is this dynamic and constantly changing process of fire consuming organic material that humans use both as a material tool and as an aesthetic medium. In both cases, we accept the loss of organic material because we value the heat, light, or aesthetic objects that we can produce with its help. The burning piano forces us to look at the loss of organic material that we accept or sacrifice. When fireplace logs are burning, we might only enjoy the product of warmth and heat. When cities, forests, and living beings are burning, we would only focus on destruction, pain, and danger, and, as Davies points out, we might want to rush to help and save what can be saved, if possible. The burning piano, however, becomes a mechanical object that is somehow close to a human being; it sets destruction, affective response, and aesthetic experience into oscillating ambiguity.

Thus, the fire and the piano foreground a process of radical mediation in Grusin's sense, exposing connection and interdependence as preconditions of communication. One could say that fire and piano work as technical media of display for each other. The qualified media type of music expands into a process in which noise, sounds, and musical sounds all partake, along with human and nonhuman, organic and elemental actors. The fire and the piano play together, and the fire allows the piano to sound independently from human manipulation. An instrument considered to be defunct, in the qualifying standards of music, provides the possibilities for this elemental or even radical performance—one last, grand show without a human performer. From a posthumanist perspective, this self-consumption might signal the inevitable decline of humankind already built into the human project, in Claire Colebrook's sense,[21] or simply indicate a necessary humbling of human ambition on a heating planet.

Piano Garden

Lockwood's *Piano Garden* includes the simple instructions to "not protect against weather" and to "leave the piano(s) there forever."[22] The nineteen-minute film version from 2021 (1:11 to 1:30) transmediates this work in a wooded area of Katonah, north of New York City, where the Caramoor Summer Music Festival has run since 1945. Well-heeled listeners flock to the outdoor pavilions and Italianate villa rooms to hear the world's top musicians play innovative programs that, at the same time, continue the received practices of classical performance practice. Festival curator Stephan Moore has recently included Lockwood's work as part of an effort to open up this practice to include more multisensory and experimental sound experiences.[23]

The *Piano Garden* film focuses on the score's documentary aspect with fairly seamless time-lapse editing of still shots; it shows the piano on a series of warm, windless days, with fast-growing bushes and creepers overtaking it. In what looks like a neglected garden corner, the *material modality* features a Knabe baby grand (a more workaday model than the music festival's Steinways) surrounded by plants such as oak, maple, wild balsam, and dog rose. A keyboard performance by Madison Greenstone (normally a clarinetist), with additional sound by Stephan Moore, is not shown but heard as a nondiegetic soundtrack. The film's edits show the deserted piano throughout summer months in a series of fixed shots lasting ten to twenty seconds and separated by black frames; the sound creates continuity across the film's breaks.

In the *sensorial modality,* vision and hearing thus remain disconnected throughout the film. The piano varies among three camera positions: a medium shot showing the keyboard, a full shot from a distance showing the baby grand slightly to the right, and a shot from above foregrounding the raised lid and the piano's weathering process. The lid's upper layer has become delaminated, and one can imagine the hammer mechanisms inside the case have worn loose as well in changing weather. The keys' surfaces lie scattered in increasing disarray throughout the film; a slight mossy layer on the varnish spreads as well (e.g., 1:18:20) (Figure 3). Other visual indications of growth and decay are very slow; in fact, they are hardly noticeable from frame to frame, except by the growth of the surrounding plants. Wild balsam grows in from the right until it covers half of the piano in the film frame, and one wild rose branch gradually invades the piano's interior (1:13:29).

Along with the visual repetition of static slightly changing images, we hear an evolving sonic improvisation (offscreen, as a soundtrack) that begins with a loud thump in the keyboard's bass range and continues as

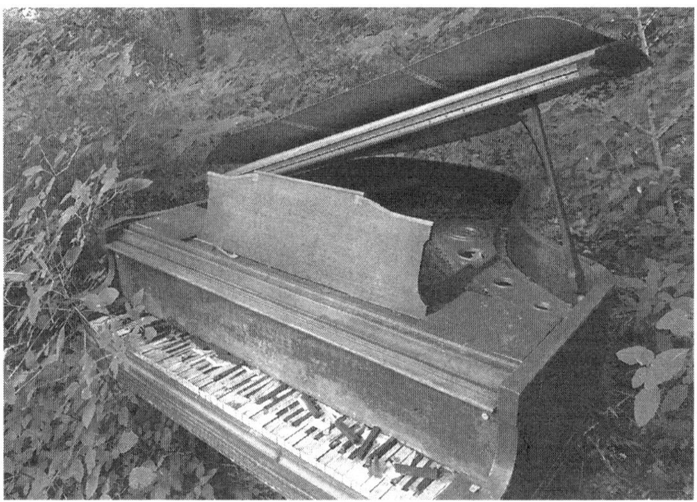

Figure 3. Annea Lockwood, *Piano Garden,* 2021. 01:21:50: The lid's upper layer has become delaminated, the keys' surfaces have become disordered, and moss has begun to spread across the varnish. Caramoor Center for Music and the Arts. Image courtesy of ISSUE Project Room.

a kind of testing of pitches and intervals, as a piano tuner would assess an instrument. The sound is not simply out of tune but also heavily influenced by the piano's mechanics breaking down, the result of changing weather and New York's high summer humidity. The improvisation seems to occur more as listening and response than as intentional sound-making. First the (invisible) players focus on the keyboard, as pitches split between the tap of each key's mechanism and the twang of loosening wires, until hardly any tone emerges from the hammers. Then the players move into the body of the piano, using extended technique to pluck and strum the strings, which sound (for a while) more in tune than when struck by the hammers. Gradually even this sense of scalar order collapses, and the players find new freedom in making faster, more aggressive, and more rhythmic sounds that exploit the piano's remaining percussive integrity. Some hammers still hit the strings; some keys produce only muffled thumps and thuds. These sounds reveal the instrument's materials that often sound individually: the soundboard, copper wires, wooden hammers, and other felt and wooden surfaces. We hear birds in the background and at some stage the faint sound of plants in the breeze. The improvisation breaks off suddenly at the end of the film, as if in midthought, while the plant growth continues its slow work to overtake the piano.

While the installation of a planted piano in the garden is stable in place and evolves over a much longer amount of time than the twenty minutes of film, the static images document consistent outdoor conditions: cloudy summer weather. The amount of documented time is left unclear. The recurring shots from similar angles create a cyclical pattern that suggests regular (weekly, monthly, annual?) visits, although this might not reflect the actual artistic process. The repetitive, static images with minimal plant movement convey a sense of timelessness in the *spatiotemporal modality*. The invisibility of the performer or performers and the lack of a clear sense of when the musical sequences were recorded creates an uncanny, acousmatic effect, implying indirectly that the sounds come from (or have come from in the past) the piano pictured in the still shots on-screen.

In the *semiotic modality*, the piano sounds offer some associations with harp glissandi, piano-tuning intervals, and occasionally syncopated rhythms. These sounds also evoke extended technique, but overall, they are more exploratory, directed by the material preconditions of this specific piano in a specific moment or moments. Visually, the film includes several iconic relationships, such as the delamination of the lid cover, which recalls the "wing" term for a grand piano in German *(Flügel)* and thus adds to a sense that the instrument becomes more creature-like when placed outdoors. *Piano Garden* also evokes a metaphorical relation to plants (in the loose key surfaces' resemblance to the disarray of autumn leaves) and, in its static and repetitive editing, a slow, plantlike experience of time.

By extending this temporal perspective through elemental and radical media, *Piano Garden* shows a piano decaying as days and even months pass in the film. As John Durham Peters has noted, humans use the sky and its movements for orientation; "sky media" are means for a sense of control over time and space.[24] Time-keeping tools such as calendars and clocks, or orienting tools such as towers and compasses, use the area above the ground to map a comprehensible, human here and now. The planted piano may not be a sky medium in Peters's sense, but it could be a case of orientation and timekeeping having moved from observation of the sky outdoors to subsidiary tools, such as clocks, which today are integrated in nearly all types of digital devices.[25] In this respect, and paradoxically, the planted piano *destabilizes* orientation in space and time. It questions the indoor/outdoor order and offers a different relation to time, not of timekeeping but as a documentation of a slow change. Instead of the short-term passing of time normally made audible by a piece of music performed on the functioning piano, this piano confronts the audience with the indefinite, slow, and often ungraspable *longue durée*—not of human history but of natural processes. For a while, even for years, the piano will still look like a musical instrument but is part of a long decomposition process, which will end when the decaying wood has turned into soil. In this way, the elemental mediation of a weathered piano exposes the time stretching that occurs in musical performance (think of the length of a song versus spoken text) but in a more ecologically embedded, less linear way. While music is a means to make the passing of time audible, the planted piano connects to much longer time scales, not unlike John Cage's *Organ2/ASLSP*, which has been continuously performed in Halberstadt, Germany, since 2001 and will take 639 years.[26]

After analyzing *Piano Garden* through the media modalities, our overall sense is that the planted piano shows human control loosening from its own construction. The piano's mechanisms disintegrate and sounds controlled by conventional scales collapse, remaining in this decomposed state long enough to reveal the piano's materiality and the unexpected sounds formed by its environment. The displaced, decaying piano also calls attention to the constant changes and unpredictability of outdoor weather that we try to control and model as best we can.[27] When humans stop trying to control a piano's physical environment, we risk entropic loss in the face of heat, cold, humidity, and other forces. The process recalls Caitlin DeSilvey's point that when humans ask "certain buildings, objects, or landscapes to function as mnemonic devices" for cultural value, we assume the need to protect them. *Piano Garden,* then, confronts us with the alternative: to refrain from intervening and allow for processes of "erosion, weathering, decay, and decomposition."[28] The piano is subjected to the same slow process of decay and in-betweenness of a dead forest tree trunk. While decomposing into soil from which new plants can grow, the dead wood offers a habitat for numerous living beings, showing how deconstruction or decomposition is part of biological cycles. Even if we want to protect the piano from change, this is not the natural state of things but rather the result of human control.

Piano Drowning

Piano Drowning (ISSUE Project Room 1:30:00 to 2:30:00) documents a 2021 performance that features a commissioned piece by Welsh composer Ynyr Pritchard in performance with Xenia Pestova Bennett at Plas Bodfa, Wales. Though Annea Lockwood's score for this work does not include instructions for a live performance (aside from playing the instrument once a month), this iteration includes a sheet music score and prepared piano objects. The piece is entitled "Boddi," meaning "to drown or swamp." Apart from the drowned piano on which the piece is performed, the title also refers to the controversial 1965 flooding of a rural community in Wales to create a reservoir and provide water for industry in Liverpool.[29] Four artist-observers were also invited to respond to the piano, the composition, and the natural environment.[30] While the performers observe some concert conventions, the long lead-up to their playing becomes just as important, as an open surface (not unlike the "silence" of John Cage's *4′33″*) on which random images, sounds, and conversations occur.

Piano Drowning transmediates a variety of possible spaces, objects, humans, and nonhuman beings in the *material modality.* The film zooms in and out among a meadow landscape, a grove between the meadows, and a pond within the grove. Within these environments one notices plants (e.g., meadow flowers, willows, reeds, water lilies), animals (birdsong, cows, fish), artistic material (pens, pencils, colors, paper), and technical equipment (microphones, cameras, cables, computers), as well as people standing, sitting, strolling, and chatting, with two visual artists and two musical performers. An upright piano has already been placed in the pond, close to its edge in the grove of trees. Thus, the film presents the piano as only one object in a larger ecosystem. Sound engineers and camera operators also appear in the film. One could even mention the water's surface as a participant—not only as a mirror for objects and living beings but also as a medium of display for sunshine, wind, and rain.

The film calls attention to the *sensorial modality* but blocks familiar forms of perception. The first succession of shots (a rural landscape from above including a small grove, then a pond in a grove, and finally a close-up of a water lily in the pond) recalls nature-film rather than performance conventions. The editing oscillates between frequent close-ups to wide shots—for example, from the close-up of a microphone in the open piano lid with hammers exposed (1:31) to the pond with the piano placed inside (1:32:16 to 1:37:25). Thus, the piano appears simultaneously embedded and deterritorialized in a natural habitat. Even the mirroring water surface destabilizes vision—for example, by showing only the mirror image of a leg upside-down (Figure 4, 1:49), or showing reeds reflected on the motionless pond so that the line between air and water disappears (2:21). Not only is the piano mirrored in the pond, but the qualified media type of film also mirrors itself in the editing process. Camera operators (1:32) and sound engineers (1:35:26) are the first human figures to appear (Figure 5), and later a sound engineer directly meets our gaze (1:50:24). A visual focus that switches between details and wholes is accompanied by the *sounds* of murmuring human voices, footsteps, and remote traffic sounds, as well as the noises of cows, chickens, and waterfowl. These sounds, for instance footsteps in the grass, often proceed the sight of the action, as in a person walking through the meadow (1:37:55 to 1:38:04). Sounds and images are presented as related but remain disconnected. For instance, we see a piano mirrored in the motionless surface of the pond while we hear splashes of wading feet; we hear murmured comments about recording quality close by, and shortly afterward we see from across the pond a sound engineer stepping into the water to adjust a microphone. It takes a while to realize that disconnected nearby sounds and images shot from a distance might show the same or a similar event (1:34:32 to 1:35:26). At other times, we hear sounds and see images from different events. We hear the discussion of the musical performance while we see an artist drawing, or we see people talking while we hear a different conversation (1:48). This lag creates a temporarily acousmatic, disorienting effect, in which the source of a sound is not clear, adding to the off-kilter quality of the film. This deliberate lag also exposes the artificiality of audiovisual events in film, as they are often created for seamless effect from disparate images and sounds. Here the device is bared in a Brechtian mode of defamiliarization, calling attention to what audiences usually take for granted.

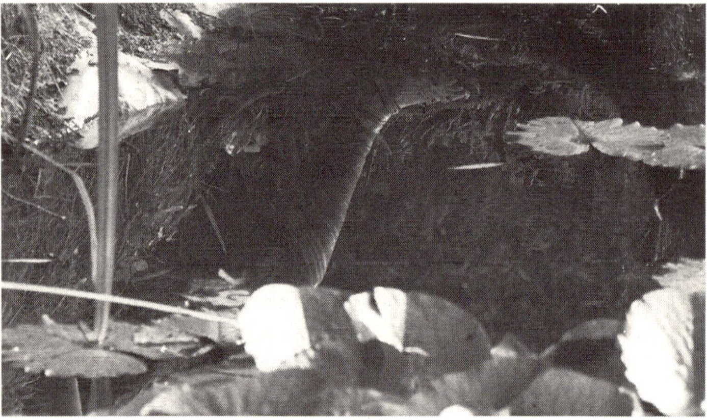

Figure 4. Annea Lockwood, *Piano Drowning,* 2021. 1:49: Close-up of a leg mirrored in the pond. Presented by Soundlands and ISSUE in Plas Bodfa, Wales, photo by Jonathan Lewis. Image courtesy of ISSUE Project Room.

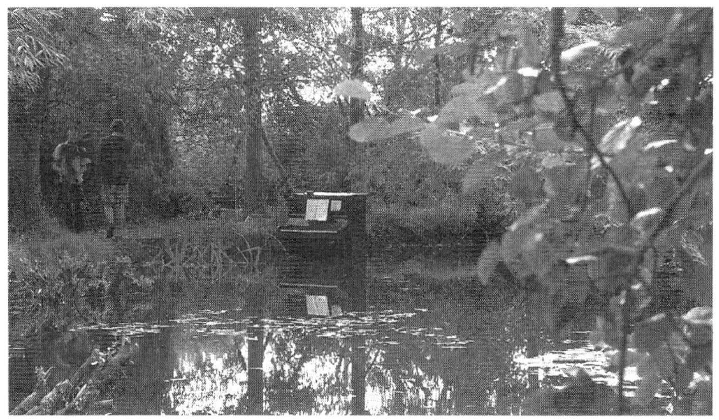

Figure 5. Annea Lockwood, *Piano Drowning,* 2021. 1:34:55: Piano mirrored and camera operators visible. Image courtesy of ISSUE Project Room. Presented by Soundlands and ISSUE in Plas Bodfa, Wales, photo by Jonathan Lewis. Image courtesy of ISSUE Project Room.

In the *spatiotemporal modality,* close-up shots (of usually a minute) by a fixed or only slowly moving camera encourage the viewer to switch focus and discover new, unfamiliar sights within the same frame—for instance, the veins of water lily leaves that protrude in the sunshine (1:41:29) or water pooling in the middle of another leaf, the curves of its surface tension, and a refraction of light (1:51:26). Sometimes, it is the camera lens that switches focus between different objects (e.g., 1:38:05 to 1:39:24). The constant shifts between close-up and wide-angle shots create a peculiar rhythm and an implicit sense of movement between the shots. There is no stable point of view and no clear sense of time, as the sequence of images is not always in chronological order; the piano appears sometimes with a score and sometimes without (1:41:20) with people moving or with the pond deserted, in bright sunshine, or with raindrops disturbing the pond's mirror surface (1:47). Here even nature-film conventions unravel, as the scene is temporally unpredictable and the visual focus wanders. Together with the long waiting period between the beginning of the film and the actual piano performance, this editing style creates a discomfiting experience of time, as viewers may impatiently expect the piano to make sounds and begin to wonder if it will ever happen at all.

In the *semiotic modality,* the first part of the film foregrounds the detailed iconicity of images, particularly in the close-ups. The way hearing precedes vision foregrounds the indexical quality of sounds and their mysterious, acousmatic potential. Less stress is on conventional signs as the film subtly destabilizes perception and orientation. Even the performance of "Boddi" is embedded in close observance of nature, as the camera zooms in on rings on the water (1:57:50), before we see, one after the other, the boots, legs, and rest of the performers' bodies. The performers are clothed not in concert dress but in fishing pants and athletic wear. They wade to the piano and take position in front of the keyboard and at the back of the piano, with hands in the open lid: they stand there, motionless and silent for around a minute. They play, or rather manipulate, the piano not only with their hands but also with a bicycle tube, a megaphone, a comb, and a mallet.

While the camera and the sound of the recording are now synchronized, the performance artificially disconnects piano-playing conventions. When the performance starts, however, audio and video need to be synched. The performance itself keeps the film's disjunction present in other ways. In the typical treatment of a piano, the manipulated keys and strings are mechanically connected. In this case, their sounds are split from each other. We see one pair of hands moving on the keyboard and hear the wooden mechanism; we also hear another pair of hands strumming the strings with a comb. The hand movements on the keyboard are conventional as patterns for scales and chords, with low, rhythmic repetitions not unlike the *Winnsboro Cotton Mill Blues* style played in *Piano Burning.* In another sense the performance recalls extended-technique piano performance, as the musicians stroke the keys toward the body, hammer with flat hands and later with fists and arms, or play the piano's internal wires and wooden parts. The camera documents the performers' movements, zooms in to show hands on the keyboard (according to the conventions of filmed performance) but also zooms out into the landscape (2:03) and below the water surface via a muddy underwater shot (2:09).

The film defamiliarizes the piano's sounds in several ways. The performance starts with the piano's hammer mechanism sounding separately from the copper wires, each treated by a different pair of hands. These string sounds are not what one would expect from a piano, although the strumming of the highest wires (around 2:03) sounds nearly as if the keys were pressed. The reason for the muted sound, which one first might think is the result of the piano placed in water, is later revealed as a bicycle tube. When it is removed, the first, musical sounds of a rousing folksong melody create a bit of a shock (2:04:32). Even in this case, conventional piano sounds occur via isolated piano mechanisms—the sound of wooden keys clicking, or the wires strummed and hammered, the pegs struck producing bell-like overtones, or the wooden surfaces resonating with a howling sound. With this variety of unexpected sounds, the piano takes on an almost feral quality. The performers continue to play the instrument in different ways, alternating sounding and muffled keys via the keyboard and the internal wires. As an electronically amplified body made of wood, the piano gains a human voice when the second performer (the composer, Ynyr Pritchard) screams sentences in Welsh through a megaphone into the piano, which is "answered" by the instrument with the feedback loop when the megaphone is held behind the soundboard.

The performers play for 18 minutes; their motionless standing at the beginning and the end (and to mark a second part in the piece) recalls conventions of marking a performance space and time. However, there is no applause or sound of the audience leaving; the performance simply merges into the surrounding soundscape. Distant traffic and machines, birdsong, humming insects, cries of waterfowl (2:26), and cows are part of the soundscape again, together with images of the piano from different perspectives mirroring the pond. The last shot, of nearly three minutes, shows the piano in receding light (it might be evening). Its motionless quiet draws attention to the sounds of traffic, birdsong, occasional footsteps, and an airplane until the fade-out (2:30), but the soundscape of traffic and birds continues to sound during the end credits.

In the *semiotic modality* of the performance itself, *Piano Drowning* foregrounds the indexical relation of sounding objects and materials, with occasional iconic or associative aspects, such as the cotton-mill pattern, the sudden melody, and rhythmically struck octaves recalling the sound of bells. At the same time, despite including elements that the audience might recognize, the work defamiliarizes established conventions. Though the performative space and time are carefully set by the motionless standing of the performers at the beginning and the end, what is seen and heard in between is disconnected and complex. The aggressive performativity of the piece may relate to the "Boddi" drowning of the village, which Welsh listeners would associate with the music's title, especially as Tryweryn was one of the last Welsh-speaking communities in the country at the time.[31] This history also complicates the pastoral scene of this *Piano Drowning* iteration, as the act of flooding a town may create a beautiful, watery landscape, but in its cost to human and nonhuman communities for the sake of industrial production far away, the act takes on a sinister quality.

If this performance were to take place in a concert hall, its prepared (as in the bicycle tube), "inside," and extended-technique aspects might be expected in a twentieth-century or contemporary program. But outdoors in a pond, in a performance with no set starting time, even the performers' use of sheet music becomes defamiliarized. The film's oscillating near–far dynamic, combined with the contrast of familiar and strange sounds, creates a constantly shifting perception. Objects appear upside down or inside out, but in an interconnected way. Viewers can appreciate and connect with the unfamiliar not as a disruption but as an extension of what sounding materials can mean. The piano itself becomes an unstable element in a larger ecosystem, with implicit references to historical and environmental loss. Thus, the drowned piano in the pond, the performance of "Boddi," and the film's documentation enact a complex interplay of different parts, senses, and actors that we usually perceive as a whole, such as "a piano," "a musical performance" and even "nature" and "culture," by disconnecting, zooming in and out, creating audiovisual lag, and baring a relational network that we usually ignore.

On the elemental-media level, when John Durham Peters explores water as a medium, he approaches oceans as environments for cetaceans—mammals adapted to a life underwater that inverts all the conditions of land-living creatures. Water creates a sonar environment with altered sense ratios, where sound travels faster than sight and where sound, not sight, is the sense that connects and orients across distance.[32] Liquid environments invert inside and outside, sight and sound, organs and the senses, above and below, ground and fluidity, and thus also highlight how human bodies, perception, thinking, craft, and media all are shaped by adaptation to earthly environments.

Piano Drowning conveys some of the destabilizing potential of water as an element and its capacity to transgress boundaries. The pond is not a natural habitat for the piano, just as a piano placed in the garden and submitted to weather becomes endangered and fragile. In the context of "Boddi," this displacement also signals the loss of human culture—not in a positive, posthumanist way but in a traumatic historical sense. This semiotic addition also highlights the potential for life-threatening floods in a time of global heating. Like the piano pushed into the street during a California landslide or the pianos flooded or crushed in Appalachian homes during Hurricane Helene, more and more human cultural materials will likely be drowned (and not by choice) in the near future.

At the same time, *Piano Drowning* offers a new, upside down perspective through the medium of water that mirrors, inverts, and opens up the environment. Reflective tension between the familiar and the unfamiliar makes itself noticeable when we engage with the drowned piano, be it by performance or filmic documentation. The water's surface makes wind and rain visually perceptible, but it is a surface that, contrary to human-made surfaces, mirrors while also being penetrable. Water physically connects piano, plants, and beings; its surface is not only self-reflective but opens up; it can be entered, passed through (similar to the meadow) as an interface between habitats above and below. In Gaston Bachelard's terms, water has a different reflective quality than that of a human-made mirror: "Water becomes heavier, darker, deeper; it becomes matter."[33] In a poetic sense, water also transforms at the elemental level: it is "an invitation to die . . . a special death that allows us to return to one of the elementary material refuges."[34]

The drowned and decomposing piano is no longer primarily a sounding object but first of all becomes an image (both literal and poetic). This image is mirrored and deepened by the water as an element in which various meanings can be imagined and elemental transformation can eventually occur. When the piano in the ISSUE Project Room film sounds, it needs human intervention, amplification, and even distortion. The film documentation picks up the audiovisual-disjunction characteristic of life underwater; this "microscopically small lag time" in fact only extends the slight delay between speech and hearing that occurs on the ground too, "but our senses are too dull to notice."[35] This delay becomes more obvious as the film editing estranges our normal ability to create cohesion out of different visual and auditory events. The water's surface thus also mirrors the self-reflexive character of film and the physical conditions humans usually depend on to connect with their environments. The piano in the pond creates a new perspective, defamiliarizing and fluid, as frames leak into each other and as meanings waver.

As in the other Lockwood films discussed here, *Piano Drowning* destabilizes musical conventions in favor of a more ecologically embedded approach to the piano. Our three-part analysis has traced the ways in which transplanted instruments invite an embodied response not only to music but also to the larger environment, as is doubly mediated in film. Annea Lockwood's *Piano Transplants* treat each instrument as a defamiliarizing presence, revealing elemental and radical elements of mediation that are not about communicating a message but about connectivity and response to the environment. Fire, air, and water expose materials and structures in the background. In return, the instruments make visible our related materiality formed by the elements that we usually encounter either as domesticated tools or as unleashed, violent forces. The peculiar combination of instruments and elements invites an ambiguous form of perception. We might identify with the threatened piano, but really we engage with the environment more as fire does: in constant need of fuel and oxygen, in each of our cells as well as in the larger world.

In addition, Annea Lockwood's *Piano Transplants* radically destabilize the expected human position of being in control. While classical music is especially dependent on intricate instruments and skilled musicians, these performances ask what happens when we get out of control, discover new interplay between human-made material and nonhuman actants, and take a step to the side and listen. This helps audiences inhabit the posthumanist perspective, permitting them to move toward a more entangled way of looking at the world—and to a deeper awareness of the elemental climate changes that will inevitably affect cultural materials. The kind of embodied experience offered by *Piano Transplants* is not an easily decoded message but a shift that occurs slowly, by engaging with these artworks over time.

5 FROM DAMAGE TO SALVAGE

Instruments for Listening

IN THE COURSE OF THIS BOOK, we have shown how decomposing pianos can change human perceptions of what an instrument is and what it can do. This is not simply an invitation to burn more pianos but a shift toward greater awareness of instruments as media, which aids in a posthumanist decentering of artistic conventions and binaries like in tune/out of tune, sound/noise, and human/nonhuman. The slowness of watching and listening as a piano burns, decays, or drowns invites more curiosity about musical materiality and the agencies of fire, plant growth, air, and water in creating entangled, sounding bodies.

In this chapter, we share examples of contemporary instruments as sites of ecological embeddedness and more-than-human listening. We aim to show how current musical explorations move beyond the concert hall and encourage deeper sonic responsiveness to the world. This mode of listening reduces investment in human ego and perfectionism in favor of what the Romantics valued as "the unpredictability and complexity of nature" as mediated by such instruments as the aeolian harp.[1] While we do not advocate a naïve return to an aesthetic past that idealized "Nature" as if uninvolved with human activity, and while we appreciate the sheer difficulty of escaping anthropocentric thought,[2] we do find that ecologically enmeshed instruments invite more open, curious human responses. As John Durham Peters notes, a medial perspective can be a step toward posthumanist awareness, which acknowledges the massive impact humans have had on the nonhuman while at the same time involving and connecting other forms of life.[3]

Stefan Östersjö has claimed that "a musician's listening is shaped by musical instruments"—for example, a pianist's attunement to the diatonic scale or a percussionist's awareness of rhythmic patterns in everyday life.[4] This observation supports intermedial and elemental media points about bodies and objects in relationship. Outdoor listening amplifies this relationality, as we hear more than what instruments direct our ears to notice. In fact, this situated experience is more than hearing; we're also perceiving the whole "weather-world" in which "light, sound and feeling tear at our moorings just as the wind tears at the limbs of trees rooted to the earth . . . sweeping the body up into their own currents."[5] The unpredictable effects of weather, as kairos or "season-time" in Heidegger's sense,[6] are even more noticeable when they touch musical instruments. Musicians asked to play for outdoor weddings or sporting events are familiar with the challenges of keeping instruments in tune. Even brass instruments respond to weather; the metal can shrink slightly in cold temperatures, affecting tuning, and their keys and valves can rust in condensation.[7] Musicians playing wooden string instruments know that joints and soundboards can contract, warp, crack, or split in cold weather, a problem sometimes solved in the use of less sensitive instruments, such as carbon-fiber harps. But while these more tonally reliable instruments have practical use in high humidity or even in a hot-air balloon,[8] they do not connect to the natural environment with the individual sonority, sensitivity, and capacity for decay that wooden instruments do.

In the previous chapter, we focused on forms of mediation in Annea Lockwood's *Piano Transplants.* That analysis has formed a bridge toward understanding the entangled relationships of other unconventional, outdoor instruments. We focus here on contemporary string and wind instruments sounding through organic matter and weather, primarily in work by Östersjö, his students, and collaborators, and by performance artist Julia Adzuki. These instruments invite situated listening not through destruction or decay but through inventive work with wood, strings, or clay and the elements they meet. The projects we discuss here build on the experimental spirit of works like *Piano Transplants,* with a greater emphasis on mediating relationships between human and material and between structured instruments and unpredictable natural forces. We conclude the chapter with an artistic research reflection on coauthor Heidi Hart's *Harp Transplant* after a year in the changing weather of the southeastern United States (including Hurricane Helene in 2024), with additional attention to this project's unexpected intersection with sound art in Tehran.

Aeolian Guitars and Floating Violins

Within a wide range of ecologically involved musical practices, from Vienna's Vegetable Orchestra (involving actual vegetables) to jazz improvisations with whales, Stefan Östersjö's outdoor instruments work more as sensors than as performative tools. They reveal a similarly unpredictable "weather-world" attunement to that of Annea Lockwood's *Piano Transplants.* The point of these sonic interactions is not renaturing or decomposition for its own sake but rather setting up a relationship in which elemental forces can work acoustically through the instruments' materials, keeping their human players in the background. A 2013 experiment with a "floating guitar" strung with fishing line, for example, called attention to air as sonic presence, as the "aeolian sounds from the guitar blend with the rich soundscape of water and land . . . [in] a transmodal experience of the instrument and the place."[9] A 2014 video of the Landscape Quartet (Östersjö with Bennett Hogg, Matthew Sansom, and Sabine Vogel) shows four human figures on the edge of Klagshamns Udde, a marshy peninsula near Malmö, Sweden. They stand (mostly) still in the wind, holding a flute, a guitar, and several violins at slightly changing angles. The current at their feet rolls out into the Sound between Sweden and Denmark as their instruments hum and sing in the wind. Sometimes the strings sound like fingernails on piano wires, sometimes like a human vocal trill; the flute makes a low, tremulous whistle as Vogel holds it upright in the foggy breeze. Seagulls call in the distance. At certain points, the strings' pitches match in a ringing that spreads up and down the scale. In the video, the human figures fade out of the scene, leaving only the instruments' aeolian sounds and the calling of birds, then return as ghostly outlines. Mediated through microphones and video editing, the short film evokes contingent human presence in a liminal environment, with instruments acting more as transponders than performance tools.[10]

These works rely on nonhuman forces and aeolian effects, which can sound wild and strange when heard for the first time. A review of

Mats Edén and Stefan Östersjö's *Wind, Water, Strings, Bow* describes an adapted guitar hanging from a tree, with the "extended timbre" of "wind roaring through the strings" like a feral chorus blending with the sound of running water.[11] In a broad sense, aeolian processes involve air shaping the surface of the earth—not only by erosion but also through the changing patterns that wind creates with snow or sand. Thus, wind becomes perceptible by visually or sonically engaging with its environments. The wind's effect when howling in our ears, or in the rhythmic patterns of snapping flags—these are the same processes that humans harness in wind instruments, guiding air streams to resonate. While wind instruments contain a column of air, set into vibration by the player blowing into or over a mouthpiece, air in the outer environment is what activates aeolian instruments, setting strings into vibration without human touch or whistling through an open tube. When the wind engages strings, it creates uncanny effects because these sounds are unpredictable, usually in the background, and attuned to the physical world in ways humans often forget. Eerie sheets of sound result from overtones triggered by air currents, creating what Lawrence Kramer calls an "acoustic surplus."[12] As intervallic relationships that form familiar chords (octave, fifth, and third), overtones or harmonics can sound when released by human musicians—for example, when a harpist places the heel of the hand halfway up a string and plucks a bell-like tone from a halved-again distance above with the thumb. When the wind sets overtones in motion, the sound is less controlled and creates more of a sighing or humming effect; the human player is out of the picture, allowing elemental forces to mix sounds that might or might not be heard as music. Though some disagreement persists among physicists, this effect results either from an "aeroelastic" action of strings snapping back, as in the sound of humming power lines, or from the "Kármán vortex street effect," in which the wind "sheds" spiral patterns along individual strings, releasing spontaneous overtones.[13] The sound can begin as a vague ringing that sometimes builds into masses of chime-like tones. Listeners may be surprised at the almost animal quality of the sound, like strange voices linking instruments to earth in unexpected moments.

Aeolian sounds, specifically the aeolian harp as a human-made instrument manipulated and played by the wind, have long been a source of literary and musical inspiration, from the famous biblical Psalm 137, in which the exiled Jews hung their harps along the river in Babylon, to ancient Greece (in instruments named for the wind god Aeolus), and later through the Romantic period in Europe, when Chopin's Etude Op. 25, No. 1 imitated the rolling sounds of an aeolian harp at the mercy of the wind. An aeolian guitar might call up different associations with popular music or folk-music festivals, but the sounds of its wind-activated strings are similar to those rolling through a harp on a windy day. Artistic interventions like Östersjö's foreground the material bodies of the instruments themselves as subjects interacting with wind or water rather than objects to be played according to a written score or chord sheet.

In his floating and aeolian sound works, Östersjö seeks to break down traditional distinctions between "music as sound and as structure," between "inner hearing and concrete listening," and between "expert" and "amateur" listeners, favoring instead "oscillating" acoustic awarenesses in which subjectivity and materiality are intimate, unpredictable, and closely related to their shared milieu.[14] Working collaboratively with Bennett Hogg in the Landscape Quartet, Östersjö has questioned the role of string instruments in the "cultural construct" of the concert hall, preferring to treat a violin as a "sensor in the environment," placing microphones inside it and dragging it through the woods or extending it with fishing lines and "a hazel stick wedged under the fingerboard" to create "a kind of harp."[15] Placing guitars and violins in trees, partly as sculptures (which do decay like Lockwood's pianos) and partly as aeolian instruments, Östersjö and Hogg have noted the challenges of registering sound through instruments that are as "limited" in pitch range as they are "rich" in unpredictably complex sounds.[16] In a similar project, Ontario-based Jurgita Žvinklytė and Matti Palonen have constructed "tree harps" by attaching strings to the resonant chambers of dead trunks and finding that "each tree makes a unique sound."[17] Weather affects these outdoor instruments as well. While bowing strings with twigs in a Landscape Quartet improvisation one winter day, Bennett Hogg started to notice "fine, hard crystals of snow" making a "precise ticking sound" on the violin's body, as well as noticing that "snow falling on the instrument also falls on us,"[18] creating equal reciprocity between musical and human bodies. When engaging directly with water, as in a

2013 experiment with "river violins" and guitar, the collaborators found that in addition to the aeolian sounds of the currents over the violins' extended strings, microphones attached to the instruments encouraged a kind of "micro-sonic listening" that required making choices later in the recording studio about how to relate to the river itself as a "massive, constant drone."[19]

If wind, snow, and water work as elemental media through the human-made medium of a stringed instrument, this complex is an example of what John Durham Peters calls "ensembles of natural element and human craft" or "infrastructures" that are not simply "vessels" but also, following Friedrich Kittler, work as "ontological shifters."[20] Ecologically attuned musical instruments offer not just novel sounds but also new possibilities for being and meaning that occur through changes in perception. Rachel Carson once noted that although humans have evolved so they can no longer live in the ocean, we can still "re-enter it mentally and imaginatively."[21] Though Carson was thinking of cameras and other devices that mediate watery environments through sight, a musical instrument can help us to hear our way into other habitats—or even the watery worlds of creatures related to our ancient evolutionary past. As Melody Jue has put it in her approach to "blue" or water-based media, "sensing devices . . . teach us just how entangled in the ocean we already are."[22] Close listening, further mediated by microphones, can change how instruments sound when embedded in new environments, thereby amplifying the instruments' role as ecologically sounding bodies. Bennett Hogg's violin strings start to sound contingent when in water, more like a "flute or chamber organ," depending on the tension of the strings and the speed of the current.[23] The sheer difficulty of entering and staying in a river while manipulating instruments prevents easy romanticizing of these projects; the musician "stumbles and splashes" in "an acute experience of cold and wet."[24] The sounds of the instrument reflect back to the performer (who is just as much a listener) the day's conditions in a particular environment.

Using aeolian instruments as sensors is in fact not new; an Italian abbot strung wires from his house to a nearby tower in Milan in 1785, listening for the whine of the wind when the "weather was about to change."[25] Romantic poets and scientists became curious about the

"Aeolian Harp" (as in Coleridge's 1795 poem) as an indicator of vibration, as a site of sounding and listening, as a metaphor for the human nervous system, and even as a "model for a human/mind body conceived as a machine for translating sensory vibrations into consciousness."[26] A strange collapse of the subject/object binary occurs when the sounding agent also becomes a listening, or at least a transponding, one. This form of reciprocal attunement is what musicians like Östersjö seek to enact and document, however awkward the human splashing in a river or the playing of violin strings with twigs in the winter cold. What results is not just a performer with an instrument; "the constellation of *wind-tree-strings-guitar-performer* thus becomes an eco-system" as the wind affects the strings and the human player "adjusts to the direction and force of the wind."[27] As Thoreau described the aeolian sounds of a telegraph wire, "the fibres of all things have their tension, and are strained like the strings of a lyre."[28]

Flutes as Instruments for Listening

String instruments are of course not the only means of creating ecologically attuned sound. Östersjö's collaborator Sabine Vogel has worked with metal, wooden, and clay flutes, as well as stones and microphones, as sounding bodies *(Klangkörper)* to interact with wind, water, and plants. She brings her background as a "classical plus" musician, working in jazz, punk, and free improvisation, and in sound design for a film company into her work, which is based more in questions than in product-oriented performance. "How does the weather affect a flute?" she asks as she focuses on "tuning in" to the edge of a lake, to leaves and wind, and to long grass that she has played in tandem with her human-made instrument.[29] Listening to horsetail grass through the medium of the flute (as an aerophone with a specific channel for air), Vogel became interested in how the grass itself would sound. The resulting recording ("catch the horsetail," 2012) uses a *bansuri* (Indian bamboo flute) with an internal microphone, "a new instrument—kind of a horsetail flute, that reacted on blowing and fingering" to yield breathing, clicking dynamics in tandem with a Northumberland meadow.[30] This instrument sounds different from a flute played only by human breath, just as an aeolian harp or guitar does not sound like predictably plucked or strummed strings, turning sonic expectations inside out.

Vogel's approach is not limited to "pastoral" environments, however. Like Katt Hernandez, whose PhD project (advised by Östersjö) traces ghostly urban soundscapes in Stockholm's gentrified areas, Vogel works with city histories as well. Taking inspiration from the old clay factories outside Berlin, where the bricks that built the city include flutelike holes, Vogel and her collaborator, Ute Wassermann, have played clay flutes in air and water, specifically in an aquarium. In their filmed performance *Schwebeteilchen* (2023), the musicians make percussive as well as pitched sounds with the clay flutes, which; when submerged and amplified in the aquarium, begin to resonate in surprisingly metallic, aeolian-like sounds. With the image of human hands rising and falling in the water, manipulating flutes and hydrophones, and as the clay flute bodies breathe and bubble underwater, the viewer-listener may sense a hidden layer of the city coming back to life. In this approach, similar to that of artists Anna Orlikowska and Sarina Scheidegger, who use ceramic vessels "with their own frequencies" to resonate in water,[31] musical materiality "returns clay to earth" in a reparative move.[32] Instead of human harnessing of air or water through instruments, these works show elements and materials form situated ensembles that take on sounding lives of their own.

With clay or bamboo flutes placed underwater, or with different sizes of flutes wedged in the ground so that the wind can blow through them, Vogel's work recalls not only ancient instruments using water to move sound waves and the many efforts of humans to imitate or interact with birdsongs but also Indigenous American and Sufi ideas of a flute as a body with its nine openings, separated from its origins in the reedbed. By returning the flute to the ground or water, the musician performs an act of ecological repair. To quote the Sufi poet Rumi on the sound of flutes and strings: "and if the whole world's harp / should burn up, / there will still be hidden instruments / playing, playing."[33] This apocalyptic vision of burning in the form of a harp, however metaphorical, shows how powerful musical instruments are in imagining ecological relations. Likewise, Vogel's renatured, "hidden" flutes do more than simply experiment with wind, plants, and water. They are reembedded in the source materials of their ancient forms. Drawing on her experience in Australia, learning to slow down in the Aboriginal "dreamtime" model of ecological attunement,[34] Vogel's work with these instruments helps to shift perception away from sensational or perfectionist performance and toward slow, close listening to subtle sounds that surround us, whether in a wetland or a city.

The act of making a flute from unconventional organic materials is another way to engage with sound in an embodied, renaturing way. In a 2023 workshop in Växjö, Sweden, visual and performance artist Julia Adzuki introduced the "ovular flute," an instrument made from ostrich eggs purchased from a farm outside Stockholm. Participants worked with these surprisingly strong hollowed-out eggs, forming a mouthpiece made of seashell and reed in a delicate gluing process, using sandpaper to smooth the main opening so the reed's angle would make a clear, deep tone, and finally drilling a row of holes in the eggshell to change pitches with the fingers. The materials' shapes and slipperiness made the flute-making more challenging than it might first seem, with each egg balanced on a paper cup during the mouthpiece-making process. By blowing into the eggs, listening, and responding with sandpaper to adjust the reed's angle, participants found that they were "tuning in" (to use Vogel's term[35]) rather than simply playing to make sound. Instead of mapping each flute's holes according to a given pattern, participants worked by listening and experimenting to find the sonic intervals that sounded most clearly and fit the fingers most naturally.

While taking turns with the drill, workshop participants could also explore additional instruments that Adzuki had brought with her. These included a bone harp shaped like a harness to be worn across the shoulders and played on either side of one's head, so that the player can hear the strings' resonance, regardless of whether an audience is present, and several large gourds to be worn *on* one's head, with rattling reeds suspended in the line of sight—a zone for listening and touching as the "hat" and "veil" respond to the body's movement. The bone instrument's structure also relates to each human body's shoulder blades, spine, and skull, as a reminder that the body itself is a resonating instrument. Because of the way bone conduction occurs through the skull, the instrument wearer hears and feels vibrations more strongly than others do in the room. Adzuki's workshop took on an atmosphere of curious play as participants tried on these instruments as body extensions, tested sound and response, and laughed as the usual earnestness of musical performance fell away. When the ovular flutes were mostly complete, participants tested different fingerings to find provisional scales. Closed eyes helped in shaping the warm tones that the angled mouthpiece made possible. Unlike learning to play a recorder as children in school, the players learned simply by doing, testing the size of the holes against their breath and body position, with the kind of reciprocal attunement that Östersjö's and Vogel's instruments encourage as well.

All of these instruments in the workshop space enacted the body-extension idea that we have explored here with reference to burning and drowning pianos, but in a more literal and intimate way. While organically made instruments such as the "pumpkin drum" or "carrot marimba" played by the Vegetable Orchestra in Austria might seem gimmicky, their origins in the earth (or in the body of an ostrich, as in Adzuki's ovular flutes) give them a fragility and relatedness that remind us how close even a sophisticated grand piano is to forest and ground, with its maple, mahogany, copper, and iron. Snake rattles inside Appalachian fiddles or experiments with beehives inside pianos create a similar, surprising intimacy, reframing the instrument as a habitat as natural as a dead tree while changing its sounds along with creaturely humming and buzzing.[36] Likewise, while breathing into a flute made from an egg, the human player may experience a perceptual shift: the instrument is not just a tool for sound but a material, mediating link between our species and others.

The Resonating Tree

One of Julia Adzuki's instruments links piano back to forest in a radical way. *Resonant Bodies,* a work originally designed for the hearing and sight impaired to be able to feel sonic vibrations, is made of a large ash tree trunk strung with twenty-one piano wires. Adzuki tunes the copper wires to resonate along the C-scale overtone series (the octave, fifth, and third intervals that occur in regular ratios and that manifest in aeolian effects). The instrument, shown in Figure 6, is long and deep enough for a human body to fit inside; Adzuki encourages people to crawl in, close their eyes, and experience vibration activated by plucking the

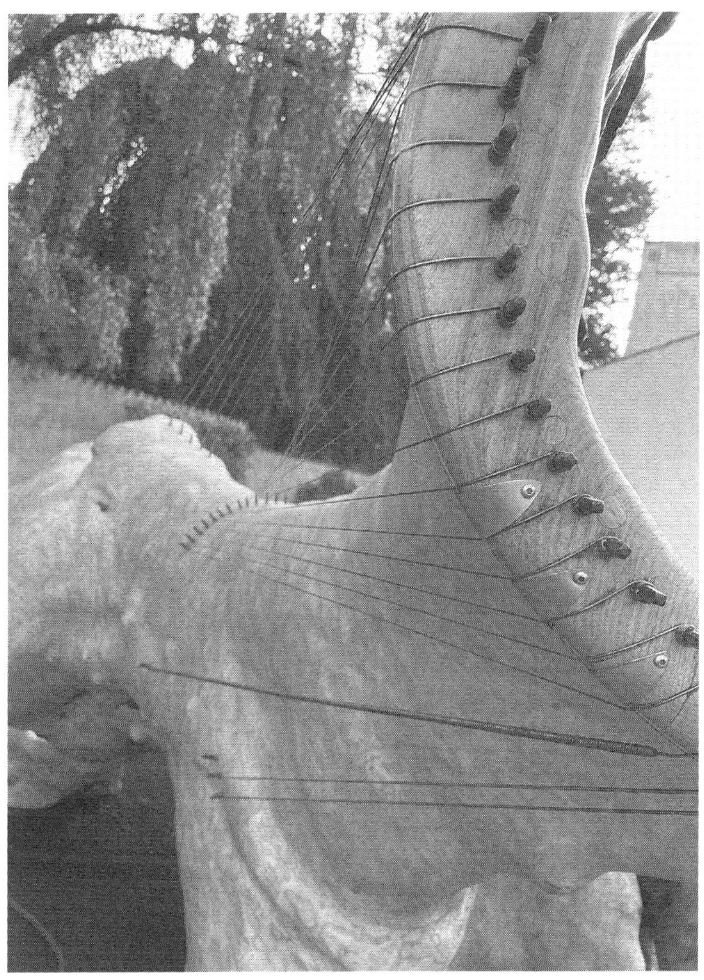

Figure 6. *Resonant Bodies* by Julia Adzuki. Ash tree trunk with twenty-one piano wires.

strings or by striking the tree's exterior with a mallet. Exposing piano wires on the outside of the tree trunk, rather than keeping them hidden, as they would be in the body of an upright or a grand with the lid down, demystifies the idea of piano and at the same time creates a new, wilder version of the kind of mechanism one might play at home. Inserting the human body into an instrument (an inversion similar to that of a flute submerged in water) also shifts conventional ideas of what it means to play or listen to musical sounds. By feeling as well as hearing the sound waves released from the wires and by touching the smooth, vibrating wood, participants become conductors of sound as well.

Like a piano, the *Resonant Bodies* instrument is as heavy and unwieldy as it is delicate. For a 2022 climate grief event in Copenhagen, a Lost Species Walk through the park-like Assistens Cemetery, Adzuki and her partner-collaborator, Patrick Dallard, brought a large trailer, which created a challenge in finding city parking, and a cart to hold the instrument while being pulled in the procession. During pauses in the walk, participants, locals who happened to be walking in the cemetery, and landscape workers took turns plucking the wires, climbing inside the instrument, drumming on its exterior, and placing their ears against it to hear as well as feel its vibrating resonance. Like the other instruments discussed here, the tree invited a playful rather than perfectionist approach to music-making (there is no one correct way to play the strings or strike the tree's surface), as well as ambiguity between performance and exploration. The low, humming, open intervals of the piano wires invited everyone to slow down and listen as well as experiment with the tree-instrument's sounds. This oscillating change in perspective echoes Stefan Östersjö's sense of collapsing binaries between different listening positions.[37] In Julia Adzuki's terms, what tree-instrument player-listeners experience is an "accord of inner and outer landscape."[38]

In her book *The Second Body,* Daisy Hildyard notes that "in normal life, a human body is rarely understood to exist outside its own skin" but that "climate change creates a new language, in which you have to be all over the place. It makes every animal body implicated in the whole world."[39] Hildyard is thinking in particular of the petrochemical extensions of human and nonhuman experience, but the idea of a second body connected to the wider world is also helpful in thinking of musical instrument extensions and the perceptual shifts they invite. During the Lost Species Walk, participants (even those who had never planned to find themselves lying inside a giant ash trunk) discovered permeable boundaries between themselves and the tree, between their own skin and the surrounding environment, and even between the living and the dead buried all around them. Experiencing vibrations through the whole body, in connection to a tree transformed into an instrument—or a more-than-instrument—made everyone a human medium as well, hearing, feeling, and transmitting sound waves. The idea of a *piano* radically renatured into a tree's body, which itself mediated live vibrations even in its dead state, thereby shifts the sense of what is possible to salvage, even as much of the world we know is at risk. At the end of the procession, Julia Adzuki passed out acorns for participants to plant.

Harp Transplant

In response to works like Lockwood's and Adzuki's, coauthor Heidi Hart has experimented with a harp transplanted into her garden in North Carolina, in the southeastern United States. Though a harp is clearly not a piano, it is closely related to that instrument in its scalar structure and its shape that mirrors the piano's cast-iron frame. In fact, the harp inside a piano has been known to serve as an instrument in its own right, notably in the Marx Brothers' 1937 film *A Day at the Races,* in which Harpo Marx breaks a piano apart as he plays "Wreckmaninoff" and then pulls out the harp from inside.[40] Planting a harp outdoors recalls Lockwood's *Piano Garden*—as if the piano's interior had already been exposed.

Using a posthole digger, Heidi's husband prepared the red-clay ground at the foot of a cherry tree. The Gothic harp that Heidi found to plant is slightly smaller than her indoor harp of similar design; it is used and of lesser quality, if not entirely "defunct" in Lockwood's terms. All of its strings are nylon, not the organic sheep gut or minerally based wound steel used in the middle and low ranges of more expensive harps, but the sounding body is made of walnut, with metal fasteners inside the soundboard to which the strings' external pegs attach. This particular model does not have feet and would normally depend on a player's body to balance it while playing. In a posthole in the garden, it is stable enough to stay upright in heavy wind, rain, leaves, ice, heat,

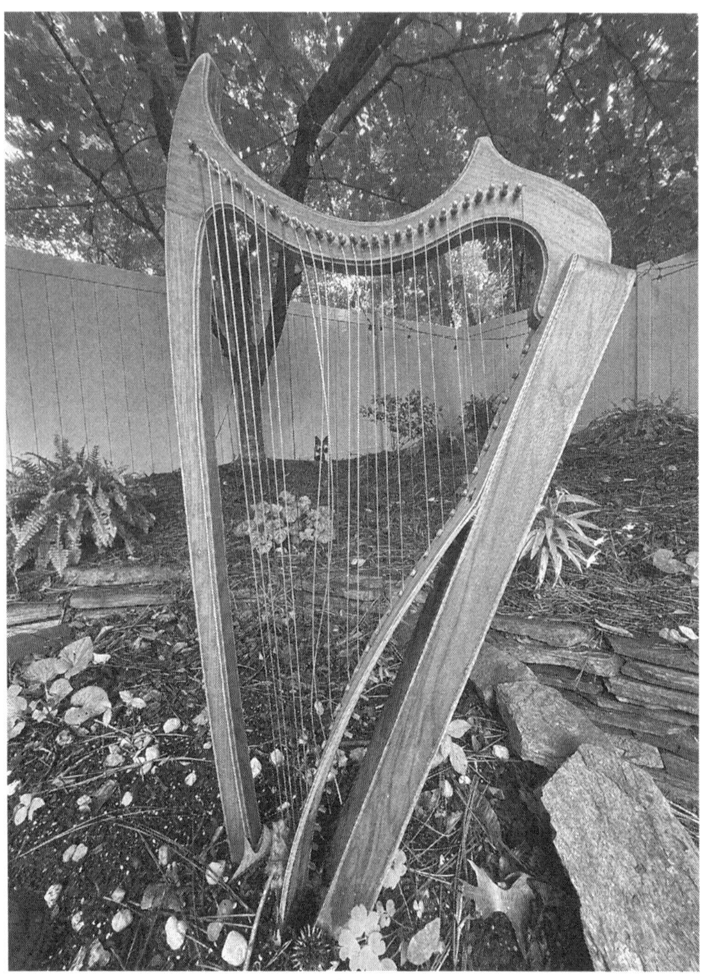

Figure 7. *Harp Transplant* in Heidi Hart's garden after one year. The strings have slackened and the soundboard separated.

and humidity—but not to withstand decomposition under these elemental conditions (Figure 7).

Heidi planted the harp in mid-April, when weather and humidity are quite variable in central North Carolina. Within a few weeks, the strings' pitches became noticeably detached from the diatonic or stepwise scale that mirrors that of a piano keyboard. Resisting the temptation to keep retuning the harp (with the truism in mind that harpists spend half of their time tuning and the other half playing out of tune, even in the best of conditions), Heidi has played and documented the harp in its process of decay through more than a year. Several months into the project, the soundboard's outer layer of wood became delaminated, leaving a gap in which spiderwebs appeared on summer mornings. Already the harp was becoming a more-than-instrument, partly in the sense of Julia Adzuki's resonating tree and partly as a kind of insect hotel. Webs between the strings became a common sight as well, especially in early fall, when orb weavers and other spiders are most active in the Southern woods. One insect, the eastern leaf-footed bug (a kind of stinkbug that looks quite intimidating when full grown), laid a perfect row of eggs along one of the harp's G strings. That these tiny brown spheres did not come loose even from the vibrating string shifted perception about what aesthetic beauty is, especially since the harp is often associated with stylized images of angels and upscale performance settings. The cyclical processes of weathering, decay, and changing habitats not only estrange the harp's conventional appearance but also reveal its biological entanglements.

In the summer's heat and humidity, the harp's strings became so de-tuned that their pitches hardly resembled a scale at all. Some lower pitches sounded higher than their neighbors; others gravitated toward the same pitch as the string next to them. Sitting down to play, Heidi found that rather than replicating known musical melodies or harmonic structures, she would respond to sounds nearby—a beeping truck in reverse, a cardinal's trilling song in a nearby tulip poplar—in another example of an embodied, situated sound ensemble. With each harp session, imitation and gesture became more important than coherent lyrical patterns. Listening to the strange detuning of the instrument, Heidi would experiment with sound cells of three or four pitches repeated up and down the harp's range (each one sounding different) or with the iconic glissandi associated with dream sequences in classic films. These ascending and descending rolls became tonally disorienting rather than associatively predictable, inviting even closer listening and decentering auditory expectations. An occasional rush of wind played with the harp, activating aeolian tremors, though not as the brilliant, rolling sounds that would occur with a harp fully exposed to the air. (This one's lowest strings are partially buried at the base.)

When the cherry, sweet gum, horse chestnut, tulip poplar, and oak trees nearby started shedding leaves in fall, some were blown between the harp strings and stayed there. Playing the even more slack, detuned strings with their leaf tangle, Heidi found that they made a metallic buzzing sound. Like the strips of paper used in some harp arrangements to evoke the sound of medieval instruments (much like the paper flapping inside pianos in Lisa Streich's *Orchestra of Black Butterflies*), and like the Appalachian snake rattle added to the interior of a violin, the leaves added a completely new sonic texture to the instrument. Heidi experimented with downward glissandi using the backs of her fingernails (an extended technique used in some legitimate harp repertoire as well) in response to this new complication. Returning to her regularly tuned Gothic harp indoors, she found that the responsive freedom of improvisation with the transplanted harp created more curiosity and freedom inside too.

After exposure to severe cold and even some rare Southern ice pellets, followed by another season of rain and heat, some of the outdoor harp's strings loosened to the point that they actually felt more like gut than nylon. They made a wavering sound when plucked, almost like a moan. The lower part of the soundboard became completely delaminated, so that light showed through the wood and the metal fasteners behind the string pegs looked like teeth inside the body of the harp. Leaves, spiders, beetles, stones, and seedlings filled in the base of the soundboard. When Hurricane Helene ravaged the mountains of western North Carolina in September 2024, the storm's edge struck the foothill region where the harp is located; heavy winds and rainfall pulled the upper strings completely away from the lower ones, leaving a gap in between and a tangle at the bottom. As of this writing, only the lowest and highest strings still sound a tone at all. In its middle range, the harp's strings sound like thrumming leather.

If the harp has been considered a somewhat mystical instrument in some cultures, this one has come down to earth like aging skin and bones. It is no longer a meticulously tuned medium for tempered scales but a radically democratic container for a wild range of chromatic, mimetic, and sometimes microtonal variation. Loosening her own ingrained ideas of musical perfectionism, Heidi has found that a dying instrument can actually foster more aliveness in playing, like Julia Adzuki's ash tree trunk. After the hurricane, the harp became an unexpected medium for climate grief; sitting down to play it brought up strong associations with far greater losses in the nearby mountains.

The transplanted harp has also made an unexpected connection with the underground sound art and musical community in Iran, where, as we have noted, instrument destruction has been anything but an artistic luxury. For the 2024 Listening Academy (hosted by the Listening Biennial) in Berlin, Heidi contributed a sound art piece combining recordings of the harp transplant and of the decayed harpsichord in her office. She was not aware that this piece would become part of a larger sound work including recordings by the group's concurrent gathering in Tehran, where musicians are acutely sensitive to the risks of their work and also to the trauma of sounds not normally associated with violence (for example, the morning call to prayer coinciding with executions).[41] At first hearing, Heidi worried that her sound work with damaged instruments would be problematic in the context of a joint listening session between the two groups, which was facilitated online. She was surprised to find that sound artist Golnoosh Heshmati had linked her piece to a recording of women weaving Kashan rugs; the sounds of percussive harpsichord keys related to the beating of the loom and a women's mourning song behind it. The additional overlap of city sounds in Tehran with the decaying harp's loosened, untuned strings—noticeable when doubly transplanted into a musical environment of microtones rather than European scales—came as another moment of surprise. This generous approach to what could easily have sounded like an insensitive insertion of artistic privilege moved the harp piece into more ambiguous spaces between music and handwork and between art and documentary sound.

This material, perceptual, and intercultural transformation shows that piano or harp transplants work as more than mere experiments.

They allow for human and nonhuman curiosity, they provide literal habitats and sonic pleasures, and in some particular cases, their sounds can even stretch across geopolitical differences to expose both the power and fragility of musical materials. As the other instruments described in this chapter demonstrate, setting a flute or guitar into relationship with water, wind, ice, or plants can cross boundaries between human culture and elemental media as well. Letting go of human control allows these instruments to whistle or moan in wild, unpredictable ways that invite closer listening to the world.

CODA

Re-membering

By re-membering throughout this book, we have traced the sonic, historical, social, medial, and ecological resonances around intentionally decomposing instruments, with special attention paid to the piano. In many cases, these once finely tuned structures undergo transformation into more-than-instruments: a habitat for insects, a water-filled case of hammers and wires, an aeolian instrument played by the wind, or a tangle of firewood. Unlike the Apple ad transforming a crushed piano into a flat, digital simulacrum, these artistic experiments are open-ended and ultimately out of human control. Unlike an expensive Fender guitar smashed in a rock concert, these instruments will not be repaired and returned to their intended cultural function. They do work as sites of imaginative ecological repair, however: returning a piano to the earth through ritual fire or water is a kind of transition from anthropocentric sound-making toward more-than-human material and sonic relations. As media in their own right, decomposing instruments also shift perspective toward materialities usually taken for granted, as in the experience of finding one's phone screen suddenly black, more matter and mirror than source of information. On another level, instruments that function as mediators, in the sense of connectors, help embody and amplify awareness of the real threats of fire and water to the world as we know it.

In their decomposition, pianos like Annea Lockwood's transplants become reembedded in biological sources and processes. Our close intermedial reading has shown not only how these works destabilize conventional perceptions of music and human culture, but also how they open new possibilities for embodied, reciprocal sound experiences. The peculiar combination of instruments and elements, as well as the interplay between human-made material and nonhuman engagement, transforms our understanding of both cultural media and nature. The burning, planted, or drowned piano highlights *Klangkörper* relationships that activate ambiguous perceptions of subject/object and of the passage of time. The artworks disrupt received expectations about cultural objects and at the same time form new connections.

The decomposition of pianos is also an invitation to *re*-compose in several senses: to improvise and make new, unpredictable sounds on a once-domesticated instrument; to reimagine human cultural materials as part of a larger ecosystem; and to re-member the power of sound to affect human and nonhuman bodies, as Julia Adzuki's tree instrument does with vibrating piano wires. Some artists have literally taken apart pianos and reordered their parts in new forms, as in the work of Jeff Bell, a sculptor whose 2013 show *RePiano* in North Carolina included a work called *Nautilus,* using a deconstructed piano's cast-iron plate as the fin of a submarine like that in Jules Verne's *20,000 Leagues Under the Sea.*[1] Works like these recall the practice of bricolage, or "fooling" in Appalachian culture, a form of "folk recycling" or "using an object to ends for which it was not intended."[2] In this context, what looks like a trash heap is really a rich field of source material. In an age when more and more pianos are being discarded or sold cheaply on social media, as burdens from a time of more ubiquitous music-making in middle-class homes, cast-off instruments offer new possibilities for experimentation and reimagining human culture.

From a posthumanist perspective, engaging with nature through instruments destabilizes the expected human position of control, often pushing the expression of cultural messages to the background. The radical letting go of valued objects from protected indoor spaces—especially when they can no longer serve their original purpose—does not merely result in a disruptive collapse of order. Instead, perception shifts from listening to music to a multisensory experience of materials, beings, and their interrelatedness. The entanglement of instruments and elements fosters symbiotic relationships, slow time, and inverted perspectives of mirroring surfaces. In this process, nature and culture are not opposed; instead, media transformation and human performance are part of a network that we usually perceive as unity, such as a musical work, a film, or an instrument.

Artists have always found methods to disrupt received perceptions and question reigning cultural paradigms. However, with posthumanist and intermedial approaches, we can trace in more detail how these radical material shifts, collapsing sensory orders, changes over time, and converging frameworks of destruction and natural processes enable new forms of more-than-human collaboration. At the very end of our project, coauthor Beate Schirrmacher had the opportunity to test this approach at a live performance of *Piano Burning* in Frederiksberg, Denmark (Figure 8). Attending an on-site performance, which we had previously analyzed through film, provided a more embodied and tactile experience, including smoke, heat, and sparks. Another striking element that Beate noticed was how the live-audience perspective heightened concern for the pianist, whose reflective playing contrasted with the quickly spreading fire. This dissonance provoked both worry and laughter amid the strange calm of the performance itself. The event's sensory variability also highlighted how film's two-dimensionality cannot fully convey the depth of space—particularly noticeable when shifting attention between *Piano Burning* photos and the live experience. Beate noticed that the audience's perception constantly shifted as well, between flames devouring the piano and the piano shaping a spectacular fire, with burning colors and smoke gliding through every gap between the keys. When one bystander remarked that "the flames are like an orchestra," the act of witnessing did in fact bear out the collapsing nature/culture binaries that we have noted throughout this book. Friends who had sounded skeptical about the idea of piano burning grew attentive to the materials, one after the other, and the overall transformational process.

Renatured and decomposing instruments do not advocate for the wholesale rejection of music and cultural heritage. Instead, these practices harness human responses to musical sounds and the instruments that produce them to engage with our environment in more attentive ways. By moving instruments outdoors and relating them with natural elements, these practices expose the distinctions humans make between what we protect and what we abandon. They also return a piano or harp to its sources in wood and metal, re-membering the instrument's body

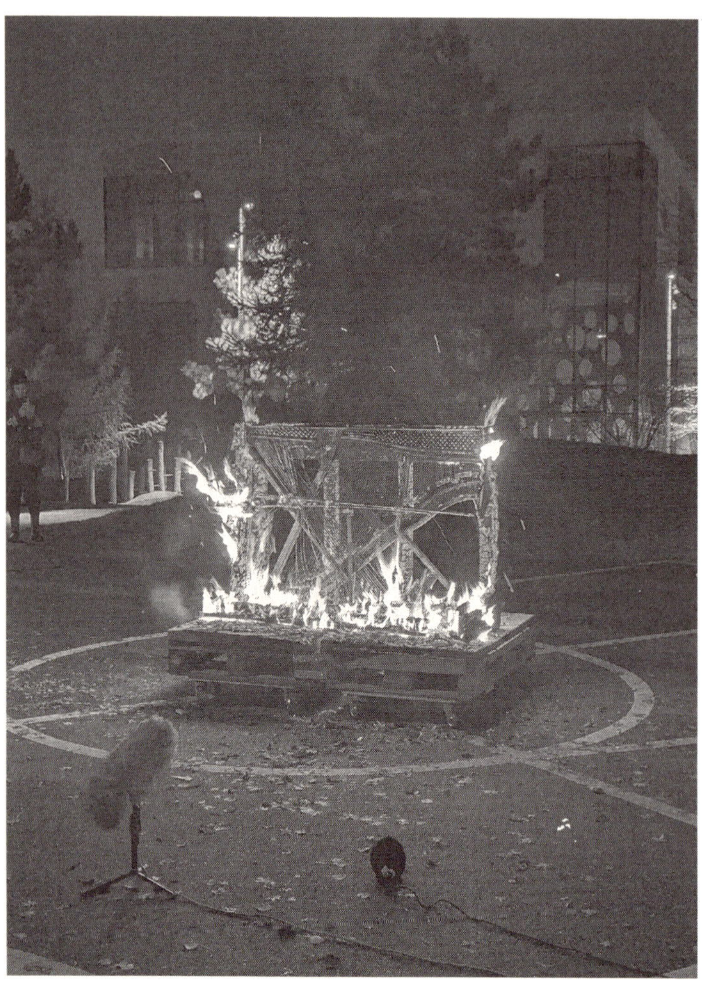

Figure 8. *Piano Burning* in Fredriksberg, Denmark. A microphone records the burning piano's sounds while the fire exposes the interior harp. Photograph by Juliane Gralle.

even as it decays or collapses in flames. This is not a binary matter and a rejection of culture; rather, these rewilded instruments highlight the value of art, using artifacts to engage with nature in less hierarchical ways. We rely on the familiar in order to understand the new; media scholars repeatedly have pointed out how new media technologies are structured on practices of old media.[3] Similarly, decomposing instruments invite us to engage with the nonhuman as attentively and curiously as we do with interfaces for human communication and culture.

As Fluxus-inspired works like Annea Lockwood's *Piano Burning* and *Piano Drowning* regain popularity in a time of heightened ecological awareness, it is important to note that these works do not celebrate instrument destruction as an authoritarian regime would or as Lady Gaga's audience did (in a completely different context) when she emerged from her own burning piano like a warrior queen. The point is not the erasure of the instrument or the empowerment of the artist, though these acts occur on opposite ends of the "sonoclasm" spectrum. Instead, a slowly burning or drowning piano becomes a medium for sensory engagement with human-made sound materials often taken for granted, reembedded in a more-than-human setting. Works like Annea Lockwood's *Piano Transplants,* along with more recent experiments using outdoor more-than-instruments, encourage deeper listening to a rich and fragile world.

As eighty-one-year-old Lockwood muses, listening to a marsh with a hydrophone in the 2022 documentary *32 Sounds,* "It's my sense that if I'm standing here, I'm just one of many organisms that are listening *with* one another . . . not even *to* the environment, we're all within it." She thinks of sound as a "sensory channel of connection" linking humans with bugs, water currents, or a passing train.[4] In the documentary, an archival film of a much younger Lockwood listening to the sound of her burning piano shows her smiling in wonder, open to whatever she might hear. In a time when long attention is becoming more difficult for humans to sustain, in our already cyborg-like linkage with devices for fast-moving sensory input, works of gradual decomposition and attentive listening serve as reminders of elemental processes to which all "vibrant matter" eventually yields.[5]

ACKNOWLEDGMENTS

This book has grown from yearslong collaborative efforts, based at the Linnaeus University Centre for Intermedial and Multimodal Studies (IMS) in Växjö, Sweden. We would like to thank IMS for ongoing support in the form of seminars, informal discussions, and Crafoord Foundation funding that has made our project possible under the title *Instruments of Repair*. This support in the form of a postdoctoral fellowship allowed Heidi Hart to work closely with Beate Schirrmacher in Sweden during the seminal period of research and writing. We extend particular thanks to IMS colleagues Jørgen Bruhn, for suggesting that we broaden the project's scope from an article to a book; Alexandra Huang-Kokina, for sharing insights about embodied piano performance; Nafiseh Mousavi, for calling our attention to examples of authoritarian instrument destruction; and seminar participants across disciplines who have provided invaluable feedback in bringing this book to fruition. We would also like to thank the musicology departments at both Linnaeus University and Lund University for inviting us to present in their seminars, and to Torbjörn Carlsson and Magnus Rydnér from the department of media and journalism at Linnaeus University for creating a public-outreach film about the project. We thank Linnaeus University Library and IMS for financial support of Open Access publication.

Many individuals have contributed to this book's formation as well: visual and performance artist Julia Adzuki, whose *Resonant Bodies* instrument is important to our concepts of instruments' materiality and who led a 2023 workshop as part of the *Instruments of Repair* project;

organist Susan Bates, harpist Catharine DeLong, and piano technician Bill Huesman for their technical expertise in instrumental structure and sound; artist-musicians Katt Hernandez, Anna Orlikowska, Sarina Scheidegger, and Sabine Vogel for sharing their practices with unconventional tunings and outdoor instruments; Brandon LaBelle and the 2024 Listening Academy in Berlin for providing deeper insights into environmental sounding and response; Golnoosh Heshmati for including Heidi Hart's sound recordings of a decaying harp and harpsichord in a politically nuanced tapestry of sound-making; visual artist Paul Travis Phillips for sharing his practice of autodestructive art through the medium of rust; and musicologists Brian Gilliam and Lawrence Kramer for conversations that have revealed that even long-established artistic practices of instrument destruction can still come as a shock. Thanks also to the 2024 Natural Resonance Festival for including this book's artistic-research component, *Harp Transplant,* in an online lecture performance.

Special thanks to this book's editor, Pieter Martin, for careful reading and clear guidance in the publication process, and to series editors Giovanni Aloi and Caroline Picard for additional feedback and support. Finally, we would like to thank our families for their gifts of listening and time, and John Halverson in particular for his efforts in transplanting a harp outdoors.

NOTES

Introduction

1. Salvador Hernandez, "A Mudslide Sent a 149-Year-Old Piano Out a Window and Into the Muck. Its Journey Isn't Over," *Los Angeles Times,* 11 March 2024, https://www.latimes.com.
2. WXII12 News, "6 Videos Show Destruction of Helene as It Ripped Through North Carolina," 27 September 2024, https://www.wxii12.com/article/hurricane-helene-video-north-carolina-flooding.
3. See Daniel J. Wakin, "For More Pianos, the Last Note Is a Thud in the Dump," *Seattle Times,* 30 July 2012, https://www.seattletimes.com/life/lifestyle/for-more-pianos-the-last-note-is-a-thud-in-the-dump; and Richard Chin, "Requiem for a Piano: Hundreds a Year Are Being Trashed in Minnesota," *Minnesota Star Tribune,* 29 March 2024, https://www.startribune.com/hundreds-of-pianos-a-year-are-being-trashed-in-minnesota.
4. ISSUE Project Room, *Annea Lockwood: Piano Transplants—Piano Burning, Piano Garden and Piano Drowning,* streaming event, 13 October 2021, https://issueprojectroom.org/event/annea-lockwood-piano-transplants-piano-burning-piano-garden-piano-drowning.
5. Peter C. Baker, "That Much-Despised Apple Ad Could Be More Disturbing than It Looks," *New York Times Magazine,* June 2024, https://www.nytimes.com/2024/06/06/magazine/apple-ipad-ad.
6. Ron Synovitz and Haroon Bacha, "Outrage Stoked by Video of Taliban Humiliating Musicians, Burning Instruments," *Radio Free Europe,* 18 January 2022, https://www.rferl.org/a/taliban-video-humiliating-afghan-musicians/31660157. See also Cameron Moody, "Iranian Music Censorship and International Law," *Brooklyn Journal of International Law* 47, no. 1 (2022),

https://ssrn.com/abstract=4208387; and Shima Shahrabi, "On Censorship, Cultural Destruction and the Power of Music," *Iranwire,* 31 August 2016, https://iranwire.com/en/provinces/63959/.

7. Céline Trachsel, "Taliban verfolgten ihn, deshalb musste Pianist Elham (16) flüchten," *20 Minuten Nachrichten,* 23 May 2024, https://www.20min.ch.
8. See Brian Moynahan, *Leningrad: Siege and Symphony* (Quercus, 2013).
9. J. Philip Newell, *Listening for the Heartbeat of God: A Celtic Spirituality* (Paulist Press, 1997), 53.
10. Dionne Brand, *A Map to the Door of No Return: Notes to Belonging* (Vintage Canada, 2011), 76.
11. Stephen Davies, *Themes in the Philosophy of Music* (Oxford University Press, 2003), 108–18; and Matteo Ravasio, "On the Destruction of Musical Instruments," *Journal of Aesthetics and Culture* 8, no. 1 (2016), https://doi.org/10.3402/jac.v8.32222.
12. Elin Kanhov, "From Birdsong to Deepfakes—Attending to Challenges for Music in the 21st Century," webinar, Posthumanities Hub, 26 September 2024. See also Anna Kirse, *Koku Opera* (2016), clip available on YouTube, https://www.youtube.com/watch?v=9zJzeWi9jSY.
13. See WARPS (World Association for Ruined Piano Studies), 2022, https://bolleter.wixsite.com/warpsmusic; and Shohei Kudo, "Nature Prepared Toy Piano," Instagram, 15 April 2024, https://www.instagram.com/shoheikudomusic/.
14. Annea Lockwood, "Bonfire of the Ivories: Visualize Your Piano—Burning," interview in *The White Fungus,* excerpted in the *Utne Reader,* 8 June 2009. https://www.utne.com/arts/bonfire-of-the-ivories-visualize-your-piano-burning.
15. Kyle Devine, *Decomposed: The Political Ecology of Music* (MIT Press, 2019), 14.
16. See Gordon Bolton, "How to Make a Difference with Eco-Friendly Piano Disposal," Piano Movers of Texas, 20 December 2023, https://pianomoversoftexas.com/blog/make-difference-environmentally-friendly-piano-disposal.
17. Annea Lockwood, artist's website, https://www.annealockwood.com/compositions/piano-transplants/. See also Culture Colony News, "Annea Lockwood's *Piano Drowning,*" 2022, https://culturecolony.com/en/news/annea-lockwoods-piano-drowning.
18. Ross Bolleter, "The Well Weathered Piano: A Study in Ruin," in *Sound Scripts: Proceedings of the 2007 Totally Huge New Music Conference,* ed. Cat Hope and Jonathan Marshall, vol. 2 (Australian Music Centre, 2009).
19. Natasha Barrett, artist's website, Acousmatic/Electronic, https://www.natashabarrett.net/acousmatic.

20. Sophy Roberts, *The Lost Pianos of Siberia* (Grove Press, 2020), 65–66.
21. Chuck Wing and Isaac Hale, "Now More Pianists than Ever Can Play Abravanel Hall," *Deseret (Utah) News,* 2 September 2024, https://www.deseret.com/utah/2024/09/02/photo-gallery-now-more-pianists-than-ever-can-play-abravanel-hall.
22. Aaron S. Allen and Kevin Dawe, eds., *Current Directions in Ecomusicology: Music, Culture, Nature* (Routledge, 2016).
23. Mark Peter Wright, *Listening After Nature: Field Recording, Ecology, Critical Practice* (Bloomsbury Academic, 2022).
24. Budhaditya Chattopadhyay, *Sound Practices in the Global South: Co-Listening to Resounding Plurilogues* (Palgrave Macmillan, 2022).
25. Salomé Voegelin, *Uncurating Sound: Knowledge with Voice and Hands* (Bloomsbury Academic, 2023), 61.
26. See Timothy Morton, *All Art Is Ecological* (Penguin Random House, 2021); and Giovanni Aloi and Michael Marder, eds., *Vegetal Entwinements in Philosophy and Art: A Reader* (MIT Press, 2023).
27. See Catilin DeSilvey, *Curated Decay: Heritage Beyond Saving* (University of Minnesota Press, 2017); Felicity Fenner, *Curating in a Time of Ecological Crisis: Biennales as Agents of Change* (Routledge, 2022); and Heidi Hart, *Climate Thanatology: Companioning What Remains* (Really Simple Syndication Press, 2022).
28. Hannah Baader, Gerhard Wolf, and Sugata Ray, eds., *Ecologies, Aesthetics, and Histories of Art* (De Gruyter, 2024); and Karl Kusserow, ed., *Picture Ecology: Art and Ecocriticism in Planetary Perspective* (Princeton University Press, 2021).
29. Mine Doğantan-Dack, ed., *Rethinking the Musical Instrument* (Cambridge Scholars Publishing, 2022).
30. Alexander Refsum Jensenius, *Sound Actions: Conceptualizing Musical Instruments* (MIT Press, 2022).
31. Aaron S. Allen, "Ecoörganology: Toward the Ecological Study of Musical Instruments," in *Sounds, Ecologies, Musics,* ed. Aaron S. Allen and Jeff Todd Titon (Oxford University Press, 2023).
32. Stefan Östersjö, *Listening to the Other* (Leuven University Press, 2020).
33. See Davies, *Themes;* and Ravasio, "On the Destruction."
34. Beate Schirrmacher, "Musical Performance and Textual Performativity in Elfriede Jelinek's *The Piano Teacher,*" in *Word and Music Studies—New Paths, New Methods* (Danish Musicology Online Special Edition, 2016); Beate Schirrmacher, "The Transmediation of Ambivalence: Violence and Music in Burgess's *A Clockwork Orange* and Kubrick's Film Adaptation," *Ekphrasis* 2 (2019): 26–40; and Heidi Hart and Beate Schirrmacher, "Music,

Noise, and Nature: Energetic Ambiguities in Benedikt Erlingsson's *Woman at War,*" *Music and the Moving Image* 15, no. 3 (2018): 3–19. See also Kanhov, "From Birdsong to Deepfakes."

35. Asun López-Varela Azcárate, "Posthuman Intermedial Semiotics and Distributed Agency for Sustainable Development," in *The Palgrave Handbook of Intermediality,* ed. Jørgen Bruhn, Asun López-Varela Azcárate, and Miriam de Paiva Vieira (Palgrave Macmillan, 2024).
36. Vadim Keylin, "Unauthored Music and Ready-Made Landscapes: Aeolian Sound Sculpture," *Gli spazi della musica* 4, no. 2 (2015), http://www.ojs.unito.it/index.php/spazidellamusica.
37. John Durham Peters, *The Marvelous Clouds: Toward a Philosophy of Elemental Media* (University of Chicago Press, 2015).
38. For a thorough discussion of "forever" waste versus regenerative composting, see Mikkel Krause Frantzen, *Klodens fald: Æsthetiske og økologiske perspektiver på olie, plastisk og andre hyperabjekter* (Laboratory for Aesthetics and Ecology, 2021).
39. In addition to Peters's text on elemental media, see Richard Grusin, "Radical Mediation," *Critical Inquiry* 42, no. 1 (2015): 124–48.
40. See Davies, *Themes;* and Ravasio, "On the Destruction."
41. Claire Colebrook, *Death of the PostHuman: Essays on Extinction,* vol. 1 (Open Humanities Press, 2014), https://www.openhumanitiespress.org/books/titles/death-of-the-posthuman/.
42. Lars Elleström, ed., *Beyond Media Borders, Volume 1: Intermedial Relations Among Multimodal Media* (Palgrave Macmillan, 2021).

1. Toward a History of Decomposing Pianos

1. Roy Heidicker, "Battle of Britain: RAF Piano-Burning Tradition," Seymour Johnson Air Force Base, 18 August 2017, https://www.seymourjohnson.af.mil/News/Commentaries/Display/Article/1282899/.
2. Ruth Jones, "Ritual, Creativity and Performance in Contemporary Art and Anthropology," LAND2 research network, University of Leeds, 2023, https://land2.leeds.ac.uk/ritual-creativity-performance-contemporary-art-anthropology/.
3. Samuel Weber, *Theatricality as Medium* (Fordham University Press 2004), 40.
4. Antonin Artaud, *The Theater and Its Double,* trans. Mary Caroline Richards (Grove Press, 1958), 31.
5. Kate MacLeod, Harpers Ferry Fiddle Day video, Facebook, 20 May 2024, https://www.facebook.com/macleodkate/videos/382084211497296.

6. Nick Hudson, "Desert Island Dissection," Nick Hudson Industries, 2022, https://www.theacademyofsun.com/post/desert-island-dissection.
7. Morten Paulsen, artist's archive, 2014–23, https://www.morten-poulsen.dk/works-and-projects-archive.
8. "Japanese Pianist Plays the Burning Piano at a Sunset Beach," Reuters, 19 March 2008, https://reuters.screenocean.com/record/231745.
9. Alcantara, "Chiharu Shiota—In Silence," 2002/2019, https://www.alcantara.com/artists/chiharu-shiota/.
10. Stefan Östersjö, *Listening to the Other* (Leuven University Press, 2020), 13.
11. Michael Hannan, "*Burning Questions:* Artist's Statement," *Earclips,* 2002, https://www.abc.net.au/rn/legacy/features/earclips/.
12. Alan Sykes, "Burning Grand Pianos on the Scottish Border," *Guardian,* 22 May 2012, https://www.theguardian.com/uk/the-northerner/2012/may/22/.
13. Michal Ben-Horin, *Musical Biographies: The Music of Memory in Post-1945 German Literature* (De Gruyter, 2016).
14. Gustav Metzger, *Damaged Nature, Auto-Destructive Art* (Coracle/Russell Press, 1996). For analysis of Metzger's work in the context of destructive art and trauma, see Kristine Stiles, *Concerning Consequences: Studies in Art, Destruction, and Trauma* (University of Chicago Press, 2016).
15. "Gustav Metzger, Whose Creations Were Works of Destruction, Dies at 90," obituary by Colin Dwyer, NPR, 3 March 2017, https://www.npr.org/sections/thetwo-way/2017/03/03/518350960/gustav-metzger-whose-creations-were-works-of-destruction-dies-at-90.
16. Metzger, *Damaged Nature,* 27.
17. Claudia Ross, "What Happens When Creation Is Destruction? The Art of Cai Guo-Qiang and Gustav Metzger," *Hyperallergic,* 5 November 2024, https://hyperallergic.com/963549/.
18. Superflex, *Flooded McDonald's,* artists' website, 2009, https://superflex.net/works/flooded_mcdonalds; Zachary Small, "Danish Artist Drowns Le Corbusier's Most Famous Building in Fjord," *Hyperallergic,* 6 August 2018, https://hyperallergic.com/453981/.
19. Donna De Salvo, ed., *Open Systems: Rethinking Art c. 1970* (Tate Publishing, 2005), 3.
20. Lucy R. Lippard, ed., *Six Years: The Dematerialization of the Art Object from 1966 to 1972* (University of California Press, 1997), ix.
21. Synnøve Marie Vik, "*Damaged Nature:* The Media Ecology of Auto-Destructive Art," in *Media and the Ecological Crisis,* ed. Richard Maxwell, Jon Raundalen, and Nina Lager Vestberg (Routledge, 2105), 11.
22. Jacques Rancière, "What Medium Can Mean," *Parrhesia* 11 (2011): 35–36.
23. Fluxusgram, "Event for the Twilight," Mieko Shiomi, Instagram, 2023, https://www.instagram.com/p/CyMNh0My6B2/.

24. Rui Eduardo Paes, "Fluxus— 40 Scores," *Wrong Wrong Magazine* 22 (2017), https://wrongwrong.net/article/fluxus-40-scores.
25. Kate Molleson, *Sound Within Sound: Radical Composers of the Twentieth Century* (Abrams Press, 2022), 302.
26. Annea Lockwood, "How to Prepare a Piano," in *Sound Scripts: Proceedings of the 2007 Totally Huge New Music Conference,* ed. Cat Hope and Jonathan Marshall, vol. 2 (Australian Music Centre, 2009), 20.
27. Molleson, *Sound Within Sound,* 276.
28. Molleson, 277.
29. Molleson, 277.
30. Soundlands, *Piano Drowning,* Plas Bodfa, Wales, 13 October 2021 and ongoing, https://soundlands.org/piano-drowning/.
31. Kieron Shand, "Annea Lockwood's *Piano Drowning,*" *Culture Colony: Vision,* 19 January 2022, https://culturecolony.com/en/news/annea-lockwoods-piano-drowning.
32. Annea Lockwood, interview, *Navel-Gazers,* 14 February 2023, https://blog.navelgazers.co.uk/2023/02/.
33. Lorie Waxman, "Selva Aparicio's Memorials to Loss and Renewal," *Hyperallergic,* 26 March 2024, https://hyperallergic.com/880247/.
34. Benning Violins, "Folk Fiddles and Rattlesnake Rattles," undated, https://www.benningviolins.com/reference/folk-fiddles-and-rattlesnake-rattles.
35. Cat Hope and Jonathan Marshall, "A New Historicism? Sound, Music, and Ruined Pianos," in Hope and Marshall, *Sound Scripts,* 6.
36. Ruth Ewan, *The People's Instruments,* solo exhibition, Denmark, 2012, artist's website, https://www.ruthewan.com/the-peoples-instruments/.
37. Art in Context, "Fluxus Movement—The Avant-Garde Fluxus Movement Explained," 9 March 2023, https://artincontext.org/fluxus-movement/.
38. Lockwood, *Navel-Gazers* interview.
39. Ruth Anderson and Annea Lockwood, *Hearing Studies* (Open Space Music, 2021).
40. David George Haskell, *Sounds Wild and Broken: Sonic Marvels, Evolution's Creativity, and the Crisis of Sensory Extinction* (Penguin, 2022), 239.
41. Vadim Keylin, "Unauthored Music and Ready-Made Landscapes: Aeolian Sound Sculpture," *Gli spazi della musica* 4, no. 2 (2015), http://www.ojs.unito.it/index.php/spazidellamusica.
42. Keylin, 74–75, 79.
43. Magda Mayas, *Orchestrating Timbre: Unfolding Processes of Timbre and Memory in Improvisational Piano Performance* (University of Gothenburg, 2019), 48.

44. Rob Sommerlad, "The Amazing Adventures of Kastner's Miraculous Pyrophone (Part One)," Science Museum blog, 9 February 2012, https://blog.sciencemuseum.org.uk/pyrophone1/.
45. Mayas, *Orchestrating Timbre,* 47.
46. Richard Hawley, "How Composer John Cage Transformed the Piano—With the Help of Some Household Objects," *Smithsonian,* 24 September 2019, https://www.smithsonianmag.com/innovation/.
47. "Rebecca Horn," The Art Story, undated, https://www.theartstory.org/artist/horn-rebecca/.
48. Anna Xambó, *De-Tuning a Tuning,* PhD website, 2022, https://annaxambo.me/music/solo-performances/.
49. Mayas, *Orchestrating Timbre,* 16, 49.
50. La Biennale di Venezia: Music, Zeno Baldi/Lisa Streich, 8 October 2024, https://www.labiennale.org/en/music/2024; Zachary Woolfe, "In the Art Biennale's Shadow, Venice Celebrates Music, Too," *New York Times,* 22 October 2024, https://www.nytimes.com/2024/10/22/arts/music/venice-music-biennale.
51. Ultima Programme, "Dancing into Fire," Oslo, 2024, https://www.ultima.no/en/dancing-into-fire.
52. See BBC On This Day, "Hitler Survives Assassination Attempt," 20 July 1944, http://news.bbc.co.uk/onthisday/hi/dates/stories/july/20; and Peter Julicher, *"Enemies of the People" Under the Soviets: A History of Repression and Its Consequences* (McFarland, 2015).
53. Naama Tsabar, *Estuaries,* Hamburger Bahnhof, Berlin, 2024, https://www.smb.museum/en/museums-institutions/hamburger-bahnhof/exhibitions/detail/naama-tsabar/.
54. Salomé Voegelin, *Uncurating Sound: Knowledge with Voice and Hands* (Bloomsbury Academic, 2023), 60–61.
55. Lockwood, *Navel-Gazers* interview.
56. Queen's University Belfast, Seminar and Concert: Annea Lockwood (featuring Xenia Pestova Bennett on piano), 21 April 2023, https://www.qub.ac.uk/research-centres/sarc/events/archive-2023-events/.
57. Annea Lockwood, "From the Banks of the River Danube: A Conversation with Annea Lockwood," interview by Daniel Beban, 2008, https://thebigidea.nz/stories/.
58. Lockwood.
59. Hope and Marshall, "A New Historicism?," 3.
60. Annea Lockwood, R. I. P. Hayman, and Gordon Monahan, discussion in "The Environment," special issue, *EAR: Magazine of New Music* 16, no. 2 (1991): 32.

61. Shohei Kudo, "Nature Prepared Toy Piano," Instagram, 15 April 2024, https://www.instagram.com/shoheikudomusic/.
62. Jackson Arn, "The Whitney Biennial's Taste for Flesh," *New Yorker,* 22 March 2024, https://www.newyorker.com/magazine/2024/04/01/.
63. Julia Krolik and Owen Fernley, *The Decomposing Piano,* 2009, https://decomposingpianos.com/trilogy/harp/.
64. Simone Keller, *Call-a-Friend Project,* Center of Contemporary Art, Tbilisi, Georgia, 4 February 2024, https://www.facebook.com/simone.keller1/posts/.
65. Susan Bates, organ demonstration, Winston-Salem, N.C., 6 October 2024.
66. Lockwood et al., discussion in "The Environment," 30.
67. Tori Wrånes, *Loose Cannon* (2010), artist's website, https://www.toriwraanes.com/loose-cannon.
68. Oscar Comettant, *In the Land of Kangaroos and Gold Mines: A Frenchman's View of Australia in 1888* (1890), trans. Judith Armstrong (Rigby, 1980), 136–37.
69. Kerryn Goldsworthy, "14th of October 1843," in *Red Hot Notes,* ed. Carmel Bird (Queensland University Press, 1996), 89.
70. Ross Bolleter, "The Well Weathered Piano: A Study in Ruin," in Hope and Marshall, *Sound Scripts,* 90.
71. Bolleter, 92.
72. Bolleter, 89.
73. Bolleter, 96.
74. Bolleter, 96.
75. Östersjö, *Listening to the Other,* 11.
76. Robert Castiglione, *The Well Weathered Piano,* documentary film, 2021, https://vimeo.com/455140930.
77. Creative Research into Sound Arts Practice (CriSAP), University of the Arts London, *Wild Energies: Live Materials* conference program, 2022, https://www.crisap.org/wp-content/uploads/2022/04/Wild-Energies-Live-Materials-Programme.pdf.
78. Bolleter, "Well Weathered Piano," 95.
79. Queen's University Belfast, 21 April 2023.
80. Neil Fisher, "Nash Ensemble Review—Searing Moth Requiem Caps a Great Birtwistle Tribute," *Sunday Times (U.K.),* 27 March 2024, https://www.thetimes.co.uk/article/.
81. Benning Violins, "Folk Fiddles."
82. See Mark A. Cheetham, *Landscape into Eco Art: Articulations of Nature Since the '60s* (Pennsylvania State University Press, 2018).

83. See Hannah Baader, Gerhard Wolf, and Sugata Ray, eds., *Ecologies, Aesthetics, and Histories of Art* (De Gruyter, 2024); and Heidi Hart, "Emergency in Reverse: Moments in Climate Art History," *Solastalgia* exhibition catalog, Kalmar Konstmuseum, Sweden, 2023.
84. Strøm electronic music site, "OPLØSNING: An Audiovisual Performance Exploring Life and Decay in a Subterranean Climate," featuring composer August Rosenbaum and visual artist Ea Verdoner, 23 October 2024, https://strm.dk/oploesning-an-audiovisual-performance-exploring-life-and-decay-in-a-subterranean-climate/.
85. Milo Juráni, "Anthropocentrism on the Stage," *Critical Stages/Scènes critiques,* no. 24 (2021), https://www.critical-stages.org/24/.
86. Vicky Angelaki, "Theatre and Environment: Crisis, Society, Representation," seminar, Centre for Intermedial and Multimodal Studies, Linnaeus University, Växjö, Sweden, 10 April 2024.
87. Brian Hioe, "A Haunting Meditation on Fukushima: Ryuichi Sakamoto's 'Is Your Time,'" *Electric Soul,* September 2021, https://www.electricsoul.com/magazine/.
88. Jill H. Casid, "Necrolandscaping," in *Natura: Environmental Aesthetics After Landscape,* ed. Jens Andermann, Lisa Blackmore, and Dayron Carrillo Morell (Diaphanes, 2018), 237.
89. Casid, 240.
90. Nils Bubant, "Haunted Geologies: Spirits, Stones, and the Necropolitics of the Anthropocene," in *Arts of Living on a Damaged Planet: Ghosts and Monsters of the Anthropocene,* ed. Anna Lowenhaupt Tsing, Nils Bubandt, Elaine Gan, and Heather Anne Swanson (University of Minnesota Press, 2017), 137.

2. Piano as Medium, Material, and Representation

1. Budhaditya Chattopadhyay, *Sound Practices in the Global South: Co-Listening to Resounding Plurilogues* (Palgrave Macmillan, 2022), 69.
2. David George Haskell, *Sounds Wild and Broken: Sonic Marvels, Evolution's Creativity, and the Crisis of Sensory Extinction* (Penguin, 2022), 239.
3. Naomi Sato, Japanese *shō* demonstration, Theatre of Voices live performance, Copenhagen, 18 May 2023.
4. Aaron S. Allen, "Ecoörganology: Toward the Ecological Study of Musical Instruments," in *Sounds, Ecologies, Musics,* ed. Aaron S. Allen and Jeff Todd Titon (Oxford University Press, 2023), 17.
5. Thomas L. Hankins and Robert J. Silverman, *Instruments and the Imagination* (Princeton University Press, 1995), 10–11.

6. Maria Grishakova, "Intermediality: Introducing Terminology and Approaches in the Field," in *The Palgrave Handbook of Intermediality*, ed. Jørgen Bruhn, Asun López-Varela Azcárate, and Miriam de Paiva Vieira (Palgrave Macmillan, 2024), 14.
7. See Gabriele Rippl, introduction to *Handbook of Intermediality: Literature–Image–Sound–Music*, ed. Gabriele Rippl (De Gruyter Mouton, 2015); Lars Elleström, ed., *Beyond Media Borders, Volume 1: Intermedial Relations Among Multimodal Media* (Palgrave Macmillan, 2021); and Jørgen Bruhn and Beate Schirrmacher, eds., *Intermedial Studies: An Introduction to Meaning Across Media* (Routledge, 2022).
8. Elleström, *Beyond Media Borders*, 46.
9. See Lars Elleström, ed., *Media Borders, Multimodality, and Intermediality* (Palgrave MacMillan, 2010); and Elleström, *Beyond Media Borders*.
10. Elleström, *Beyond Media Borders*, 46.
11. John Durham Peters, *Speaking into the Air: A History of the Idea of Communication* (University of Chicago Press, 1999).
12. William James, *A World of Pure Experience: Essays in Radical Empiricism* (Longmans, 1912), 42.
13. Richard Grusin, "Radical Mediation," *Critical Inquiry* 42, no. 1 (2015): 125.
14. Grusin, 125.
15. Grusin, 132.
16. Grusin, 129.
17. Asun López-Varela Azcárate, "Posthuman Intermedial Semiotics and Distributed Agency for Sustainable Development," in Bruhn et al., *Palgrave Handbook of Intermediality*, 1215.
18. John Durham Peters, *The Marvelous Clouds: Toward a Philosophy of Elemental Media* (University of Chicago Press, 2015), 15.
19. Peters, 8.
20. Peters, 4.
21. Peters, 127.
22. Melody Jue, *Wild Blue Media: Thinking Through Seawater* (Duke University Press, 2020), 145.
23. Azcárate, "Posthuman Intermedial Semiotics," 1223.
24. Peters, *Marvelous Clouds*, 230.
25. Peters, 230–31.
26. Stefan Östersjö, *Listening to the Other* (Leuven University Press, 2020), 13.
27. Östersjö, 21.
28. Alexandra Huang-Kokina, "Touching Through Music, Touching Through Words," *Performance Research* 27, no. 2 (2022): 50, https://doi.org/10.1080/13528165.2022.2117419.

29. Serenella Iovino and Serpil Oppermann, *Material Ecocriticism* (Indiana University Press, 2014), 8.
30. Iovino and Oppermann, 7.
31. John Koster, "History and Construction of the Harpsichord," in *The Cambridge Companion to the Harpsichord,* ed. Mark Kroll (Cambridge University Press, 2019), https://doi.org/10.1017/9781316659359.003.
32. See Stuart Isacoff, *Temperament: How Music Became a Battleground for the Great Minds of Western Civilization* (Vintage, 2001).
33. See Magda Mayas, *Orchestrating Timbre: Unfolding Processes of Timbre and Memory in Improvisational Piano Performance* (University of Gothenburg, 2019).
34. David Grover, "History of the Piano from 1709 to 1980," AMH Piano Services London, https://www.piano-tuners.org/history/d_grover.html.
35. Nicholas Giordano, "The Invention and Evolution of the Piano," *Acoustics Today* 12, no. 1 (2016): 13.
36. Bill Huesman, piano technician, interview with Heidi Hart, Winston-Salem, N.C., 6 April 2023.
37. United States Environmental Protection Agency, "Iron and Steel Foundries: National Emissions Standards for Hazardous Air Pollutants," 2020, https://www.epa.gov/stationary-sources-air-pollution/.
38. Haskell, *Sounds Wild and Broken,* 230.
39. Lawrence Kramer, *Musical Meaning: Toward a Critical History* (University of California Press, 2002), 70, 75.
40. Gillian Dooley, *She Played and Sang: Jane Austen and Music* (University of Manchester Press, 2024), 227.
41. Larson Powell and Brenda Bethman, "'One Must Have Tradition in Oneself, to Hate It Properly': Elfriede Jelinek's Musicality," *Journal of Modern Literature* 32 (2008): 172.
42. See Mary Ann Stankiewicz, "Middle Class Desire: Ornament, Industry, and Emulation in 19th-Century Art Education," *Studies in Art Education* 43, no. 4 (2002): 324–38; and Regula Hohl Trillini, *The Gaze of the Listener: English Representations of Domestic Music Making* (Brill, 2008).
43. Dooley, *She Played and Sang,* 11.
44. Arthur Loesser, *Men, Women, and Pianos: A Social History* (1954; Dover, 1990), 236.
45. Dylan Robinson, "Giving/Taking Notice," *Performance Matters* 8, no. 1 (2022): 28, https://doi.org/10.7202/1089676ar.
46. LeRoi Jones, *Blues People: Negro Music in White America* (1963; Harper Perennial, 2022), 114–15.
47. Jones, 159.

48. Heidi Hart, FAME Studios visit, Muscle Shoals, Ala., 15 April 2023.
49. Guthrie P. Ramsey Jr., *Who Hears Here: On Black Music, Pasts and Present* (University of California Press, 2022), 237–38; Brian Seibert, "With Her First Opera, Rhiannon Giddens Returns to Her Roots," *New York Times,* 19 May 2022, https://www.nytimes.com/2022/05/19/. For a perspective on reconsidering repertoire and performance practice in the United States, see Alex Ross, "Black Scholars Confront White Supremacy in Classical Music," *New Yorker,* 21 September 2020, https://www.newyorker.com/magazine/2020/09/21/.
50. See Liana MacDonald, "Silencing and Institutional Racism in Settler-Colonial Education" (PhD thesis, Victoria University of Wellington, 2017), https://openaccess.wgtn.ac.nz/articles/thesis/.
51. Dany Van Dam, "An Instrumental Thing: Pianos Extending and Becoming Postcolonial Bodies in Jane Campion's *The Piano* and Daniel Mason's *The Piano Tuner,*" in *Neo-Victorian Things,* ed. Sarah E. Maier, Brenda Ayres, and Danielle Mariann Dove (Palgrave Macmillan, 2022). For studies of narrative texts that engage with European art music as an intrinsic part of the hegemonic culture but also use it in oppositional ways, see, e.g., Christin Hoene, "Music in Contemporary Fiction," in *The Edinburgh Companion to Literature and Music,* ed. Delia da Sousa Correa (Edinburgh University Press, 2020); Christin Hoene, *Music and Identity in Postcolonial British South-Asian Literature* (Routledge, 2015); and Cameron F. Bushnell, *Postcolonial Readings of Music in World Literature Turning Empire on Its Ear* (Routledge, 2013).
52. Van Dam, "An Instrumental Thing," 94.
53. Chloe Papas, "Ebony and Ivory: A Field of Ruined Symphonies," ABC Local, 13 November 2013. https://www.abc.net.au/local/photos/2013/11/13/3890191.htm
54. Annea Lockwood, R. I. P. Hayman, and Gordon Monahan, discussion in "The Environment," special issue, *EAR: Magazine of New Music* 16, no. 2 (1991): 32.
55. James J. Gibson, *The Ecological Approach to Visual Perception,* classic ed. (1979; Taylor & Francis, 2014).
56. Stephen A. Harwood and Najmeh Hafezieh, "'Affordance'—What Does This Mean?," U.K. Academy for Information Systems Conference Proceedings, 2017, 1, https://aisel.aisnet.org/cgi/.
57. See Eric Clarke, *Ways of Listening: An Ecological Approach to the Perception of Musical Meaning* (Oxford University Press, 2004); and Tia DeNora, *Music in Everyday Life* (Cambridge University Press, 2000).
58. Dionne Brand, *A Map to the Door of No Return: Notes to Belonging* (Vintage Canada, 2011), 76, 98–99.

59. Robinson, "Giving/Taking Notice," 32.
60. Louise Erdrich, *The Last Report on the Miracles at Little No Horse* (HarperCollins, 2001), 38–39.
61. Pierre Bourdieu, *Le sens pratique* (1980), trans. Richard Nice as *The Logic of Practice* (Polity, 1990), 102.
62. Östersjö, *Listening to the Other,* 20.
63. See Chattopadhyay, *Sound Practices.*
64. Peters, *Marvelous Clouds,* 230–31.

3. Destruction, Decay, and Entangled Bodies

1. Susan Bates, organ demonstration, Winston-Salem, N.C., 29 September 2024.
2. Choe Sang-Hun, "North Korea Deploys a New Weapon Against the South: Unbearable Noise," *New York Times,* 16 November 2024, https://www.nytimes.com/2024/11/16/world/asia/north-korea-noise-weapon.
3. See John Morgan O'Connell and Salwa El-Shawan Castelo-Branco, eds., *Music and Conflict* (University of Illinois Press, 2010); Bruce Johnson and Martin Cloonan, *Dark Side of the Tune: Popular Music and Violence* (Ashgate, 2009); and Steve Goodman, *Sonic Warfare: Sound, Affect, and the Ecology of Fear* (MIT Press, 2010).
4. Theodor Adorno and Hanns Eisler, *Composing for the Films* (1947; Continuum, 2007), 47.
5. Beate Schirrmacher, "The Transmediation of Ambivalence: Violence and Music in Burgess's *A Clockwork Orange* and Kubrick's Film Adaptation," *Ekphrasis* 2 (2019): 26–40.
6. Richard Grusin, "Radical Mediation," *Critical Inquiry* 42, no. 1 (2015): 124–48.
7. Claire Colebrook, *Death of the PostHuman: Essays on Extinction,* vol. 1 (Open Humanities Press, 2014), https://www.openhumanitiespress.org/books/titles/death-of-the-posthuman/.
8. Christine Daigle, *Posthumanist Vulnerability: An Affirmative Ethics* (Bloomsbury Academic, 2023).
9. Siena Linton, "Apple Apologises for Piano-Crushing Advert—After Brilliant Bach Parody," Classic FM, 10 May 2024, https://www.classicfm.com/music-news/.
10. "Gustav Metzger, Whose Creations Were Works of Destruction, Dies at 90," obituary by Colin Dwyer, NPR, 3 March 2017, https://www.npr.org/sections/thetwo-way/2017/03/03/518350960/gustav-metzger-whose-creations-were-works-of-destruction-dies-at-90.

11. Ernie Smith, "A Brief History of Rock Stars Destroying Guitars," *Atlas Obscura,* 21 March 2016, https://www.atlasobscura.com/articles/.
12. James Montgomery, "Lady Gaga Shatters Glass, Braves Flames at American Music Awards," MTV News, 22 November 2009, https://www.mtv.com/news/ceocru/.
13. Mark Beaumont, "Jimi Hendrix, Fire Hazards and *Saturday Night Live:* Rock 'n' Roll's Raucous History of Trashing Guitars," *Independent,* 25 March 2022, https://www.independent.co.uk/arts-entertainment/music/features/.
14. Smith, "Brief History."
15. Emily Watlington, "Jesse Darling: Studio Visit," *Berlin ArtLink,* 14 May 2019, https://www.berlinartlink.com/2019/05/14/.
16. Annea Lockwood, *Piano Burning* (1968), YouTube, 2014, https://www.youtube.com/watch?v=pS5lHF-KesM.
17. ISSUE Project Room, *Annea Lockwood: Piano Transplants—Piano Burning, Piano Garden and Piano Drowning,* streaming event, 13 October 2021, https://issueprojectroom.org/event/annea-lockwood-piano-transplants-piano-burning-piano-garden-piano-drowning.
18. Mischa van Kan, commentary, musicology seminar, Linnaeus University, 5 October 2023, and Bryan Gilliam, *Harp Transplant* visit, Winston-Salem, N.C., 30 March 2024.
19. Paul Travis Phillips, studio visit, Winston-Salem, N.C., 17 September 2023.
20. Sophia Alexandra Hall, "Taliban Burns Musical Instruments in Bonfire, Declaring 'Music Causes Moral Corruption,'" Classic FM News, 1 August 2023, https://www.classicfm.com/music-news/.
21. Elizabeth Blair, "Afghanistan's Music School Falls Silent, Its Future Is Uncertain Under the Taliban," NPR, 21 August 2021, https://www.npr.org/2021/08/21/.
22. Shima Shahrabi, "On Censorship, Cultural Destruction and the Power of Music," *Iranwire,* 31 August 2016, https://iranwire.com/en/provinces/63959.
23. Cameron Moody, "Iranian Music Censorship and International Law," *Brooklyn Journal of International Law* 47, no. 1, https://ssrn.com/abstract=4208387.
24. The Listening Biennial organization hosted a shared online space for its group in Tehran and the Listening Academy in Berlin in fall 2024, making outreach and communication possible for artists and researchers in both groups; see https://listeningbiennial.net/about.
25. Nafiseh Mousavi, commentary, "De-Composing Instruments" seminar, Lund University, Lund, Sweden, 26 November 2024.

26. See Eugene Montague, "Entrainment and Embodiment in Musical Performance," in *The Oxford Handbook of Music and the Body,* ed. Youn Kim and Sander L. Gilman (Oxford University Press, 2018); and Sylvie Nozaradan, "Exploring How Musical Rhythm Entrains Brain Activity with Electroencephalogram Frequency-Tagging," *Philosophical Transactions of the Royal Society B* 369 (2014): 20130393, https://doi.org/10.1098/rstb.2013.0393.
27. Paige Pfleger, "What Music for the Dying Sounds Like," NPR, 30 July 2016, https://www.npr.org/2016/07/30/488027745/music-for-the-dying.
28. See Heidi Hart, *Hanns Eisler's Art Songs: Arguing with Beauty* (Camden House, 2018), 8–9, 58–59.
29. La Vaughn Belle, *For Alberta and Victor: A Collection of Conjurings and Opacities,* solo exhibition, The Women's Building, Copenhagen, 2021–22.
30. Fluxusgram, "Event for the Twilight," Mieko Shiomi, Instagram, 2023, https://www.instagram.com/p/CyMNh0My6B2/.
31. Christina Rees, "Notes on Christian Marclay's Guitar Drag," *Glasstire: Texas Visual Art,* 30 June 2015, https://glasstire.com/2015/06/30/.
32. Matteo Ravasio, "On the Destruction of Musical Instruments," *Journal of Aesthetics and Culture* 8, no. 1 (2016), https://doi.org/10.3402/jac.v8.32222.
33. Stephen Davies, *Themes in the Philosophy of Music* (Oxford University Press, 2003), 108–18; and Ravasio, "On the Destruction," 2.
34. Davies, *Themes,* 111.
35. Davies, 111.
36. Alexandra Huang-Kokina, "Touching Through Music, Touching Through Words," *Performance Research* 27, no. 2 (2022): 50, https://doi.org/10.1080/13528165.2022.2117419.
37. Simon Waters, "Performance Ecosystems: Ecological Approaches to Musical Interaction," conference paper, EMS: Electroacoustic Music Studies Network—De Montfort/Leicester, 2007, http://www.ems-network.org/IMG/pdf_WatersEMS07.pdf, 5.
38. Dany Van Dam, "An Instrumental Thing: Pianos Extending and Becoming Postcolonial Bodies in Jane Campion's *The Piano* and Daniel Mason's *The Piano Tuner,*" in *Neo-Victorian Things,* ed. Sarah E. Maier, Brenda Ayres, and Danielle Mariann Dove (Palgrave Macmillan, 2022), 91–110.
39. Mine Doğantan-Dack, ed., *Rethinking the Musical Instrument* (Cambridge Scholars Publishing, 2022), 3.
40. Huang-Kokina, "Touching Through Music," 51.
41. Albert Newen, Shaun Gallagher, and Leon DeBruin, "4E Cognition: Historical Roots, Key Concepts, and Central Issues," introduction to *The Oxford Handbook of 4E Cognition,* ed. Albert Newen, Leon De Bruin, and Shaun Gallagher (Oxford University Press, 2018).

42. Christoph Seibert, "Situated Approaches to Musical Experience," in *Music and Consciousness 2: Worlds, Practices, Modalities,* ed. Ruth Herbert, David Clarke, and Eric Clarke (Oxford University Press, 2019), 11.
43. See Montague, "Entrainment"; Nozaradan, "Exploring."
44. Johnson and Cloonan, *Dark Side.*
45. Davies, *Themes,* 115.
46. Davies, 117.
47. Bruno Latour, "On Actor-Network Theory: A Few Clarifications," *Soziale Welt* 47, no. 4 (1996): 370.
48. Johan Larson Lindal, "The Movement of a Musical Work: Ernst Krenek's Opus 20 in the Interwar Years" (PhD thesis, Linköping University, 2024), https://liu.diva-portal.org/smash/record.jsf?pid=diva2%3A1835846&dswid=5506.
49. Elizabeth Grosz, *Volatile Bodies: Toward a Corporeal Feminism* (Indiana University Press, 1994); and Colebrook, *Death of the PostHuman,* 124.
50. Jane Bennett, *Vibrant Matter: A Political Ecology of Things* (Duke University Press, 2010).
51. Stacy Alaimo, *Exposed: Environmental Politics and Pleasures in Posthuman Times* (University of Minnesota Press, 2016), 5.
52. Daisy Hildyard, *The Second Body* (Fitzcarraldo Editions, 2021).
53. Bruno Latour, *Reassembling the Social: An Introduction to Actor-Network Theory* (Oxford University Press, 2007), 12.
54. Latour, 46.
55. Chengzou He, "Latour's ANT Theory, New Materialism and the Future of Intermedial Studies," seminar, Centre for Intermedial and Multimodal Studies, Linnaeus University, Växjö, Sweden, 7 June 2023.
56. He.
57. Marshall McLuhan, *Understanding Media: The Extensions of Man* (McGraw-Hill, 1965).
58. Rolf Goebel, "The Soul of the Phonograph: Media-Technologies, Auditory Experience, and Literary Modernism in the Age of Covid-19," *Humanities* 9, no. 82 (2020): 6, https://doi.org/10.3390/h9030082.
59. EMBER Audio + Design visit, Winston-Salem, N.C., 19 June 2024.
60. Ravasio, "On the Destruction," 2–3.
61. John Durham Peters, *The Marvelous Clouds: Toward a Philosophy of Elemental Media* (University of Chicago Press, 2015), 163.
62. Ravasio, "On the Destruction," 4.
63. Ravasio, 5.
64. Vittoria Benzine, "Here Is Every Artwork Attacked by Climate Activists This Year, From the 'Mona Lisa' to 'Girl with a Pearl Earring,'" *Artnet,* 31 October 2022, https://news.artnet.com/art-world/.

65. Annea Lockwood, *Piano Burning* (1968), performed by clipping, YouTube, 2019, https://www.youtube.com/watch?v=2EMu15_9SF8.
66. Stuart Isacoff, *Temperament: How Music Became a Battleground for the Great Minds of Western Civilization* (Vintage, 2001), 229.
67. Aaron S. Allen and Kevin Dawe, eds., *Current Directions in Ecomusicology: Music, Culture, Nature* (Routledge, 2016), 119.
68. Cat Hope and Jonathan Marshall, "A New Historicism? Sound, Music, and Ruined Pianos," in *Sound Scripts: Proceedings of the 2007 Totally Huge New Music Conference,* ed. Cat Hope and Jonathan Marshall, vol. 2 (Australian Music Centre, 2009), 3.
69. Mikkel Krause Frantzen, *Klodens fald: Æsthetiske og økologiske perspektiver på olie, plastisk og andre hyperabjekter* (Laboratory for Aesthetics and Ecology, 2021), 112. Passage translated by H. Hart.
70. Mads Rosenthal Thomsen and Jacob Wamberg, eds., *The Bloomsbury Handbook of Posthumanism* (Bloomsbury Academic, 2020), 26.
71. T. J. Demos, *Beyond the World's End: Arts of Living at the Crossing* (Duke University Press, 2020), 18–19.
72. Scott Slovic, roundtable discussion, Environmental Humanities Conference, *Journal of Ecohumanism,* 18 November 2023 (online).
73. Peters, *Marvelous Clouds,* 4–5, 9.
74. Stefan Lorenz Sorgner, "Music," in Rosenthal Thomsen and Wamberg, *Bloomsbury Handbook of Posthumanism,* 369.
75. Sorgner, 372–73.
76. See Doğantan-Dack, *Rethinking;* and Aaron S. Allen, "Ecoörganology: Toward the Ecological Study of Musical Instruments," in *Sounds, Ecologies, Musics,* ed. Aaron S. Allen and Jeff Todd Titon (Oxford University Press, 2023).
77. Diana Coole and Samantha Frost, eds., *New Materialisms: Ontology, Agency, and Politics* (Duke University Press, 2010), 6–7.
78. Emanuele Coccia, *Metamorphoses,* trans. Robin Mackay (Polity Press, 2021), 5.
79. Donna Haraway, *Simians, Cyborgs, and Women: The Reinvention of Nature* (Routledge, 1991).
80. Coccia, *Metamorphoses,* 5.
81. Rosi Braidotti, *The Posthuman* (Polity Press, 2013), 37–50.
82. Gary Tomlinson, "Posthumanism," in *The Oxford Handbook of Western Music and Philosophy,* ed. Tomás McAuley, Nanette Nielsen, Jerrold Levinson, and Ariana Phillips-Hutton (Oxford University Press, 2021), 420.
83. Asun López-Varela Azcárate, "Posthuman Intermedial Semiotics and Distributed Agency for Sustainable Development," in *The Palgrave Handbook*

of Intermediality, ed. Jørgen Bruhn, Asun López-Varela Azcárate, and Miriam de Paiva Vieira (Palgrave Macmillan, 2024), 1223.

84. He, "Latour's ANT Theory."
85. See Bennett, *Vibrant Matter.*
86. Colebrook, *Death of the PostHuman,* 178.
87. Max Horkheimer and Theodor W. Adorno, *Dialectic of Enlightenment* (1947), trans. John Cumming (Herder and Herder, 1972).
88. Colebrook, *Death of the PostHuman,* 159.
89. Colebrook, 181.
90. Jennifer Croft, *The Extinction of Irena Rey* (Bloomsbury, 2024), 145.
91. Daigle, *Posthumanist Vulnerability,* 141.
92. Vicky Angelaki, *Theatre and Environment* (Bloomsbury, 2022), 2.
93. Samuel Barber, "A Green Lowland of Pianos," set to text by Jerzy Harsymowicz, trans. Czesław Miłosz, in *Samuel Barber: Collected Songs* (1971; G. Schirmer, 1980), 128–32.
94. Elizabeth Grosz, *Chaos, Territory, Art: Deleuze and the Framing of the Earth* (Columbia University Press, 2008), 45. Broadly put, Grosz's model posits the deterritorializing of need-driven birdsong into human musical environments rather than the movement of human cultural materials into larger ecosystems, but her model is still useful to our project in imagining movement between species and territories.
95. Daigle, *Posthumanist Vulnerability,* 7.
96. Daigle, 75.
97. Catilin DeSilvey, *Curated Decay: Heritage Beyond Saving* (University of Minnesota Press, 2017), 11.
98. Gilles Deleuze and Félix Guattari, *A Thousand Plateaus: Capitalism and Schizophrenia,* trans. Brian Massumi (University of Minnesota Press, 1987), 309.
99. Hugh Morris, "Grief, Hallucinations and Exhumed Violins: The Astonishing Music of Richard Skelton," *Guardian,* 11 April 2023, https://www.theguardian.com/music/2023/apr/11/.
100. Ruth Ewan, *The People's Instruments,* solo exhibition, Denmark, 2012, https://www.ruthewan.com/the-peoples-instruments/.
101. Allen and Dawe, *Current Directions in Ecomusicology,* 155.
102. Tomlinson, "Posthumanism," 420.

4. Media and Material Transformations

1. See Gary Tomlinson, "Posthumanism," in *The Oxford Handbook of Western Music and Philosophy,* ed. Tomás McAuley, Nanette Nielsen, Jerrold Levinson, and Ariana Phillips-Hutton (Oxford University Press, 2021).

2. Stephen Davies, *Themes in the Philosophy of Music* (Oxford University Press, 2003), 108–18; and Matteo Ravasio, "On the Destruction of Musical Instruments," *Journal of Aesthetics and Culture* 8, no. 1 (2016), https://doi.org/10.3402/jac.v8.32222.
3. Marshall McLuhan, *Understanding Media: The Extensions of Man* (McGraw-Hill, 1965).
4. See Sybille Krämer, *Medium, Messenger, Transmission: An Approach to Media Philosophy,* trans. Anthony Enns (Amsterdam University Press, 2015).
5. Eugene Montague, "Entrainment and Embodiment in Musical Performance," in *The Oxford Handbook of Music and the Body,* ed. Youn Kim and Sander L. Gilman (Oxford University Press, 2018).
6. Maddy Shaw Roberts, "New Study Finds Audience Heartbeats and Breath Rates Synchronise During a Classical Concert," Classic FM Digital Radio, 6 October 2023, https://www.classicfm.com/music-news/.
7. Lars Elleström, ed., *Beyond Media Borders, Volume 1: Intermedial Relations Among Multimodal Media* (Palgrave Macmillan, 2021), 33–41.
8. Axel Englund, *Still Songs: Music In and Around the Poetry of Paul Celan* (Ashgate, 2012), 154.
9. Davies, *Themes,* 117.
10. Richard Grusin, "Radical Mediation," *Critical Inquiry* 42, no. 1 (2015): 124–48; John Durham Peters, *Speaking into the Air: A History of the Idea of Communication* (University of Chicago Press, 1999).
11. Mikkel Krause Frantzen, *Klodens fald: Æsthetiske og økologiske perspektiver på olie, plastisk og andre hyperabjekter* (Laboratory for Aesthetics and Ecology, 2021).
12. ISSUE Project Room, *Annea Lockwood: Piano Transplants—Piano Burning, Piano Garden and Piano Drowning,* streaming event, 13 October 2021, https://issueprojectroom.org/event/annea-lockwood-piano-transplants-piano-burning-piano-garden-piano-drowning.
13. John Durham Peters, *The Marvelous Clouds: Toward a Philosophy of Elemental Media* (University of Chicago Press, 2015), 118.
14. Peters, 115.
15. Peters, 130.
16. Peters, 116.
17. Peters, 146ff.
18. Peters, 136.
19. Peters, 135.
20. Peters, 199.
21. Claire Colebrook, *Death of the PostHuman: Essays on Extinction,* vol. 1 (Open Humanities Press, 2014), https://www.openhumanitiespress.org/books/titles/death-of-the-posthuman/.

22. ISSUE Project Room, *Annea Lockwood: Piano Transplants—Piano Burning, Piano Garden and Piano Drowning,* streaming event, 13 October 2021, https://issueprojectroom.org/event/annea-lockwood-piano-transplants-piano-burning-piano-garden-piano-drowning.
23. Caramoor Summer Music Festival, "Sonic Innovations," 2023, https://caramoor.org/upcoming-events/sonic-innovations/.
24. Peters, *Marvelous Clouds,* 166.
25. Peters, 218.
26. Rob Schmitz, "A 639-Year-Long John Cage Organ Performance Strikes a New Chord in Germany," NPR, https://www.npr.org/2024/02/06/1229217832/.
27. Peters, *Marvelous Clouds,* 248.
28. Catilin DeSilvey, *Curated Decay: Heritage Beyond Saving* (University of Minnesota Press, 2017), 3–4.
29. Delyth Lloyd, "Tryweryn: Personal Stories 50 Years After Drowning," BBC News, 21 October 2015, https://www.bbc.com/news/uk-wales-34528336.
30. Plas Bodfa, *Piano Drowning,* 2022, https://www.plasbodfa.com/piano-drowning.
31. Lloyd, "Tryweryn."
32. Peters, *Marvelous Clouds,* 61–62.
33. Gaston Bachelard, *Water and Dreams: An Essay on the Imagination of Matter* (1942), trans. Edith R. Farrell (Dallas Institute of Humanities and Culture, 1983), 20.
34. Bachelard, 55.
35. Peters, *Marvelous Clouds,* 93.

5. From Damage to Salvage

1. Thomas L. Hawkins and Robert J. Silverman, *Instruments and the Imagination* (Princeton University Press, 1995), 87.
2. Scott Slovic, roundtable discussion, Environmental Humanities Conference, *Journal of Ecohumanism,* 18 November 2023 (online).
3. See John Durham Peters, *The Marvelous Clouds: Toward a Philosophy of Elemental Media* (University of Chicago Press, 2015).
4. Stefan Östersjö, *Listening to the Other* (Leuven University Press, 2020), 22.
5. Tim Ingold, *Being Alive: Essays on Movement, Knowledge and Description* (Routledge, 2011), 134–35.
6. Peters, *Marvelous Clouds,* 242.
7. Music & Arts, "How Weather Impacts Your Sound," undated, https://thevault.musicarts.com/how-weather-impacts-your-sound/.

8. David Woodworth, conversation with Heidi Hart, Heartland Harps, Zirconia, N.C., 21 December 2023.
9. Östersjö, *Listening to the Other,* 12.
10. Landscape Quartet, Klagshamns Udde aeolian performance, 2014, https://vimeo.com/91443152.
11. Mike Adcock, "Review of *Wind, water, strings, bow*" (artwork by Stefan Östersjö), *RootsWorld,* 28 April 2022, https://www.rootsworld.com/reviews/.
12. Lawrence Kramer, *The Hum of the World: A Philosophy of Listening* (University of California Press, 2018), 63.
13. Shop Smith Academy, "Wind Harp Physics," undated (archival material).
14. Östersjö, *Listening to the Other,* 30–31.
15. Östersjö, 127.
16. Östersjö, 130.
17. Chris Dart, "Tree Harps: This Duo Turns Trees into Gorgeous Ephemeral Instruments to Record Music in the Forest," CBC Arts, 14 October 2022, https://www.cbc.ca/arts/tree-harps-this-duo-turns-trees-into-gorgeous-ephemeral-instruments-to-record-music-in-the-forest.
18. Östersjö, *Listening to the Other,* 131.
19. Östersjö, 132–34.
20. Peters, *Marvelous Clouds,* 3, 25.
21. Rachel Carson, *The Sea Around Us* (1950; Oxford University Press, 1991), 15.
22. Melody Jue, *Wild Blue Media: Thinking Through Seawater* (Duke University Press, 2020), 69.
23. Östersjö, *Listening to the Other,* 140.
24. Östersjö, 141.
25. Stephen Bonner, "Aeolian Harp," Grove Music Online, 2001, https://www.oxfordmusiconline.com/grovemusic/display/10.1093/.
26. Shelley Trower, *Senses of Vibration: A History of the Pleasure and Pain of Sound* (Continuum, 2012), 13.
27. Östersjö, *Listening to the Other,* 149.
28. Henry David Thoreau, "The Telegraph Harp," journal entry, 23 September 1851, *The Blog of Henry David Thoreau,* 23 September 2014, https://blog thoreau.blogspot.com/2014/09/the-telegraph-harp-thoreaus-journal-23.html.
29. Sabine Vogel, online conversation with Heidi Hart, 7 November 2023.
30. Sabine Vogel, *catch the horsetail,* SoundCloud, 2012, https://soundcloud.com/sabine-vogel/.
31. Anna Orlikowska, conversation with Heidi Hart, The Listening Academy, Berlin, 7 September 2024. See also Anna Orlikowska, artist's website, https:

//ekwc.nl/kunstenaar/anna-orlikowska/; and Sarina Scheidegger, *Ululo-szzhhh,* performance on ceramic whistles, Instagram, 2024, https://www.instagram.com/sarina_scheidegger/p/C90D54LIWuc/?img_index=1.

32. Vogel conversation, 7 November 2023.
33. Flutopedia, "Poetry by Rumi," trans. Coleman Barks, https://www.flutopedia.com/.
34. Vogel conversation, 2023.
35. Vogel conversation, 2023.
36. Lily Hunter Green, *Bee Composed,* 2014, artist's website, https://lilyhuntergreen.com/work/.
37. Östersjö, *Listening to the Other,* 30–31.
38. Julia Adzuki, *Resonant Bodies,* artist's website, https://juliaadzuki.com/resonance.html.
39. Daisy Hildyard, *The Second Body* (Fitzcarraldo Editions, 2021), 13.
40. "Harpo Marx Plays Wreckmaninoff," from *A Day at the Races* (1937), clip available at YouTube, https://www.youtube.com/watch?v=MoTyDD0C93U.
41. The Listening Academy, Tehran and Berlin (live and virtual), 4 September 2024.

Coda

1. Jeff Bell, "Building Things from His Imagination: A Conversation with Found Object Sculpture Artist, Jeff Bell," interview by Kyesha Jennings, North Carolina Arts Council, 12 July 2022, https://www.ncarts.org/blog/2022/07/12/.
2. Rachel Wise, "Loving to Fool with Things," in *Appalachian Reckoning: A Region Responds to Hillbilly Elegy,* ed. Anthony Harkins and Meredith McCarroll (West Virginia University Press, 2019), 340.
3. See, e.g., Jay Bolter and Richard Grusin, *Remediation: Understanding New Media* (MIT Press, 1999); and Andrew Chatwick, *The Hybrid Media System: Politics and Power* (Oxford University Press, 2017).
4. Sam Green, *32 Sounds,* documentary film, 2022, YouTube movies, https://www.youtube.com/watch?v=3t1HMGVMDXY.
5. Jane Bennett, *Vibrant Matter: A Political Ecology of Things* (Duke University Press, 2010).

INDEX

HEIDI HART is arts researcher, curator, and guest instructor at Linnaeus University (Centre for Intermedial and Multimodal Studies). Her books include *Hanns Eisler's Art Songs: Arguing with Beauty* and *Climate Thanatology: Companioning What Remains.*

BEATE SCHIRRMACHER is associate professor in comparative literature in the Department of Film and Literature at Linnaeus University and a member of the Linnaeus University Centre for Intermedial and Multimodal Studies. She is coeditor of *Truth Claims Across Media* and *Intermedial Studies: An Introduction to Meaning Across Media.*